"**If** one of your goals for your child's education is for him to learn all about the 50 States, then you'll definitely want to [turn the pages of] this book! The author, Joel King, a homeschool dad has created something that will get both children and parents excited about learning the 50 states!

With 3 boys ages 5-14, I've seen plenty of curricula over the years, but this is truly the first that I've seen to take such a thorough approach to teaching the 50 states. It is just packed with information! My family absolutely loves the colorful pages with clip art and quick facts. I've never had a book that was such a complete resource. The Star-Spangled State Book gives the capital, the date the state entered the Union, the state's population and population ranking, the state's land area and land area ranking, the names of the 3 most populated cities, a picture of the state, the state flag, and then some other quick facts. That's a lot to learn, but this book will make it fun!

You won't find a more well-organized, thorough, or colorful resource anywhere. Geography and history, facts and games, all work together to make this the best US geography curriculum on the market!"

Nancy Carter, The Old Schoolhouse® Magazine

"**I** really, really like this book! I think you've got a great product! Thanks for working to make such great resources, designed especially to capture the interest of my children!"

- **Heidi Strawser**, homeschool mom

THE
STAR-SPANGLED
STATE BOOK

Have Fun
Learning About
All 50 States

by Joel F. King

Published by BRAMLEY BOOKS
A Division of Knowledge Quest, Inc.
4210 Misty Glade
San Antonio, TX 78247
www.knowledgequestmaps.com

Cover Design by Cathi Stevenson

Printed in the United States of America
Copyright © Joel F. King
All Rights Reserved
ISBN#: 978-1-932786-26-2

Illustration Credits

© 2006 Jupiterimages Corporation: pages 1, 2, 5, 6, 7, 8, 9, 10, 11, 12, 13, 14, 15, 16, 17, 18, 19, 20, 21, 22, 23, 24, 25, 26, 27, 28, 29, 30, 32, 33, 34, 35, 36, 37, 38, 39, 40, 41, 42, 43, 45, 46, 47, 48, 49, 50, 51, 52, 53, 54, 55, 56, 57, 58, 59, 60, 61, 62, 63, 64, 65, 66, 68, and 69.

Trademarks

The following trademarks were referred to in this book:
Wal-Mart® is a registered trademark of Wal-Mart Stores, Inc.
National Western® is a registered trademark of The Western Stock Show Association.
The Ford Motor Company® is a registered trademark of the Ford Motor Company.
General Motors® is a registered trademark of General Motors Corporation.
DaimlerChrysler® is a registered trademark of DaimlerChrysler AG Corporation Fed Rep Germany.
Snickers®, 3 Musketeers®, and Milky Way® are registered trademarks of Mars, Inc.

Bibliography

Information for populations were calculated by the U.S. Census Bureau. The URL address for this information is as follows: http://www.census.gov/population/projections/state/stpjpop.txt. June 1, 2006

THE Star-Spangled State Book

Turn the page to fun!

Learn about the states,

and the people that make this country great!

 Pioneers

 **Explorers**

Musicians

Soldiers

PLUS:
Games!   Quizzes!
And many, many interesting facts!

Other books in this series:

The Star-Spangled Workbook - 36 weeks of lesson plans, games, puzzles, maps and fill-in-the-blank exercises for a full year of US geography!

ISBN#: 978-1-932786-27-9

For more fun history and geography resources,
visit our website at www.knowledgequestmaps.com

INTRODUCTION

Learning about our 50 unique states will be a rewarding experience for you. However, before beginning, you may find it beneficial to read the following information.

1) Each state is listed in alphabetical order.

2) At certain places within this book, *INFO* pages have been inserted to give you a more organized look at certain important facts. (An index of these *INFO* pages can be found on the next page.)

3) Information for each state includes:
 * the name of the state's capital
 * the date that the state entered the Union
 * the state's population and population ranking
 * the state's land area and land area ranking
 * the names of the state's three most populous cities
 * a picture of the state and the state's flag
 * two stories about the state
 * a *STATE FACTS* box that contains some quick facts about the state
 * and a number in the *STATE FACTS* box that represents that state's order of admission to the Union. For example, since Hawaii was the 50th state, the number *50* will appear in its *STATE FACTS* box. To find out what the number's COLOR represents, turn to the Civil War map on page 14.

4) As mentioned before, a state's three most populous cities can be found on its *STATE PAGE*. Take a look at Alabama on page 6 of this book. Do you see *BIRMINGHAM, MONTGOMERY,* and *MOBILE*? These are listed in order with the most populous city being mentioned first. In other words, Birmingham is the largest city in Alabama, Montgomery is the second largest, and Mobile rounds out the third spot.

5) At the bottom of each *STATE PAGE* is the challenge of all challenges: the four *GEOQUIZZES*! If you want to learn more about the *GEOQUIZZES*, turn to page 5.

BEWARE!
READ THIS PAGE BEFORE CONTINUING.

2

Acknowledgements:

Special thanks to my wife and children for all of their help in making the idea for this book a reality. I also want to thank Jupiterimages Corporation for their ability and willingness to make available many of the images that have been used in this book. Also, I want to thank Heidi Armstrong for her help in editing this book.

Index to the
Information Pages

THE 50 STATES

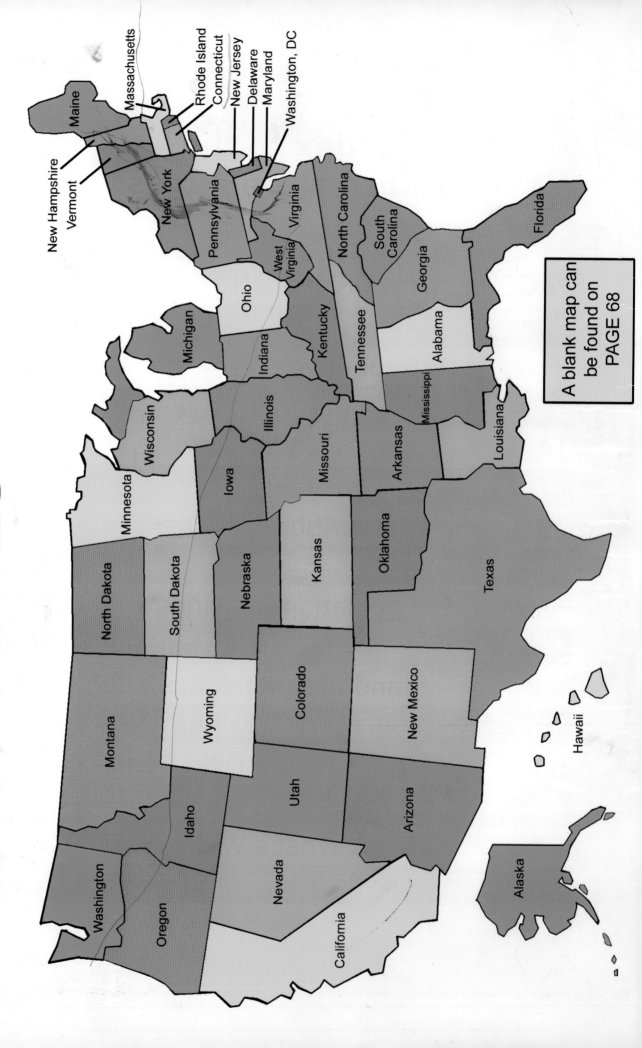

A blank map can be found on PAGE 68

The *Star-Spangled State Book* offers many ways for you to test your knowledge of the states. The *GEOQUIZ* is one of the most popular. In fact, it's so fun that we have given you four *GEOQUIZZES* to play. To play one of them, do the following:

* Pick from one of these four categories: **States, Capitals, Borders, or Trivia.**
* Look at the bottom of this page and answer that category's first clue.
* Next, look at the page number shown below your clue and turn to that page. If you end up turning to the STATE PAGE of the state that you guessed, then pat yourself on the back! You were correct. However, if you turn to the STATE PAGE of a state that you didn't guess, then you've made a mistake. Better luck next time.
* Finally, after turning to a STATE PAGE, look at the bottom of it, find your category, and continue by answering the next clue. Right or wrong, keep doing this until you've answered all 50 clues. When you've mastered the challenge, you'll make it through all 50 clues without making a mistake. GOOD LUCK!

NOTE: In order to answer ALL 50 clues, you MUST begin on this page!

STATES. CAPITALS. BORDERS. TRIVIA.

Just pick a category and begin. Read the clue.
Give your answer. Turn the pages to see if you're right!

REMEMBER: ALL GEOQUIZZES START HERE!

It's easy. If you're playing the STATES game, say the name of the state pictured below and turn to page 16 to see if you're right.

HINT: Page 16 should be Florida's STATE PAGE.

GEOQUIZ

STATES	CAPITALS	BORDERS	TRIVIA
	My capital is FRANKFORT	I border Louisiana and New Mexico.	This was the last state to be admitted to the Union.
PAGE 16	PAGE 26	PAGE 57	PAGE 18

ALABAMA

CAPITAL: Montgomery
STATEHOOD: December 14, 1819

Population: 4,631,000	Area: 50,750 square miles
RANK: 22nd	RANK: 28th

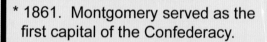

Birmingham Montgomery Mobile

ROSA PARKS

MONTGOMERY. In 1955, Rosa Parks refused to give up her bus seat to a white man. She was imprisoned and later released. However, her act led to a boycott of Montgomery's transportation system which gained much attention throughout the nation. Later, the Supreme Court declared many of the state's segregation laws unconstitutional and other stands against injustice began. No doubt, the civil rights movement owes a lot to the efforts of Rosa Parks.

22 FACTS

* 1861. Montgomery served as the first capital of the Confederacy.

* In 1902, Dr. Luther Hill performed the first open heart surgery in the Western Hemisphere. He was in Montgomery at the time.

* Sports greats Henry Aaron, Willie Mays, and Joe Lewis were born in Alabama.

* The first rocket to put a man on the moon was made in Alabama.

* People from Alabama are called Alabamians.

TRIUMPH. Blind and deaf from the age of nineteen months, Helen Adams Keller became a renowned author and lecturer. Learning to read, write, and speak in several languages, she not only was considered America's "First Lady of Courage," she became an inspiration to the world. Alabama honored Helen Keller for her ability to overcome obstacles by featuring her portrait on the backside of the state's quarter.

AL

GEOQUIZ

STATES	CAPITALS	BORDERS	TRIVIA
	My capital is RICHMOND	I border New York, Massachusetts, and Rhode Island.	The Battle of Yorktown was fought in this state.
PAGE 28	PAGE 61	PAGE 13	PAGE 61

ALASKA

CAPITAL: Juneau
STATEHOOD: January 3, 1959

Population: 700,000	Area: 570,374 square miles
RANK: 47th	RANK: 1st

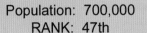 

Anchorage Juneau Fairbanks

The Great Race. The Alaskan Iditarod is a dogsled race that covers over 1,150 miles. As participants make their way from Anchorage to Nome, they must cross frozen rivers, barren mountain ranges, dense forests, desolate tundras, and windy coastlines. It's no wonder that, after facing sub-zero temperatures and blinding winds for days at a time, some consider it a victory to just reach the finish line.

49 FACTS

* In 1867, the U.S. purchased Alaska from Russia. The price was just over 7 million dollars, or about 2 cents per acre. What a deal!

* Gold was discovered in Alaska by Joe Juneau in 1880. The state's capital is named in his honor.

* Alaska is called the Last Frontier State.

* By far, Alaska has more land than any other state.

* Alaska's Mount McKinley is the tallest mountain in the U.S.

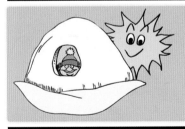

What time is it? Because of the natural wobble of the earth, the sun doesn't set in Barrow (America's northernmost city) between May 10th and August 2nd of each year! That's right, twenty-four hours of sunlight for more than 80 straight days. Then, come November, the sun doesn't rise above the horizon for sixty straight days on this city of nearly 5,000 people.

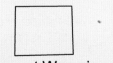
AK

GEOQUIZ

STATES	CAPITALS	BORDERS	TRIVIA
I am not Wyoming.	My capital is PHOENIX	I border North Dakota, Iowa, and Wisconsin.	The only state that I border is New Hampshire.
PAGE 12	PAGE 8	PAGE 33	PAGE 28

8

ARIZONA

CAPITAL: Phoenix
STATEHOOD: February 14, 1912

| Population: 5,230,000 | Area: 113,642 square miles |
| RANK: 20th | RANK: 6th |

Phoenix   Tucson   Mesa

ONE OF SEVEN. The Grand Canyon is considered one of the seven natural wonders of the world. Stretching for over 277 miles, Arizona's magnificent ditch has an average width of 10 miles and an average depth of one mile. So, if you plan to visit the desert state, be careful of that first step!

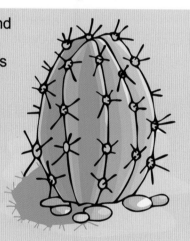

Note: In 1915, only 106,000 visitors saw the canyon. Today, more than four million people visit each year.

48 FACTS

* Arizona is known as the Grand Canyon State.

* It's hard to believe, but the original London bridge is in Arizona! It was brought to the state from England and rebuilt, stone by stone.

* Arizona produces more copper than any other state.

* The tallest fountain in the world is believed to be located in Fountain Hills, Arizona.

* At least five flags have flown over the land that is now Arizona.

TOMBSTONE. On October 26th, 1881, Sheriff Wyatt Earp and his brothers, Morgan and Virgil, met their friend, Doc Holliday, on their way to the OK Corral. Here they confronted the Clanton and McLaury gang that had earlier threatened to kill the Earps. In the historic moments to follow, gunfire was exchanged and three men lay dead: Billy Clanton, Tom McLaury, and Frank McLaury. The fight lasted about 30 seconds.

AZ

GEOQUIZ

STATES	CAPITALS	BORDERS	TRIVIA
	My capital is LANSING	I don't border any states, but I do touch Canada.	I am called the LONE STAR State.
PAGE 36	PAGE 32	PAGE 7	PAGE 57

THE 13 COLONIES

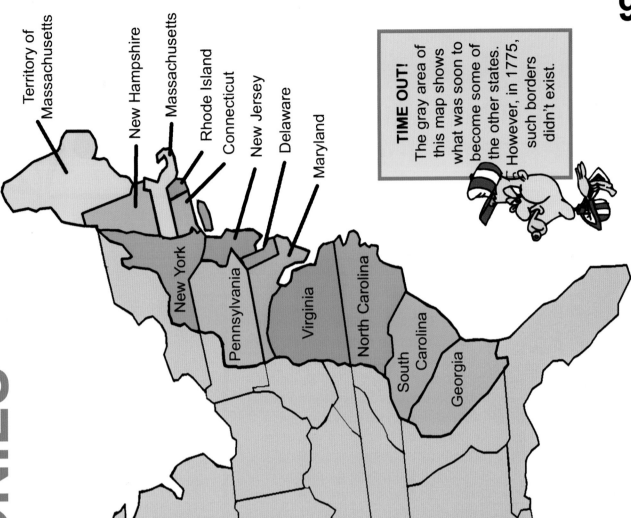

Territory of Massachusetts

New Hampshire

Massachusetts

Rhode Island

Connecticut

New Jersey

Delaware

Maryland

New York

Pennsylvania

Virginia

North Carolina

South Carolina

Georgia

TIME OUT! The gray area of this map shows what was soon to become some of the other states. However, in 1775, such borders didn't exist.

A NEW NATION. Prior to the thirteen colonies gaining their independence from England, the map of our fledgling nation looked similar to this one. Small, isn't it?

Georgia was almost half its current size. North Carolina, Virginia, Pennsylvania, and New York still had room for growth. And the lands that were to become Maine and Vermont were parts of other colonies.

Yes, the land area was small, but so was the population. Let's look at how far this nation has come.

CENSUS YEAR	POPULATION
1790	3,900,000
1820	9,600,000
1850	23,000,000
1880	50,000,000
1910	92,000,000
1940	132,000,000
1970	203,000,000
2000	281,000,000

The results are amazing. Less than 4,000,000 people were counted in the first census. Today, there are over seventy Americans for every one that existed a little over 200 years ago! And, since the beginning of World War II, the population of the U.S. has more than doubled.

ARKANSAS

CAPITAL: Little Rock
STATEHOOD: June 15, 1836

Population: 2,750,000
RANK: 33rd
Area: 52,075 square miles
RANK: 27th

Little Rock Fort Smith Fayetteville

Bill Clinton

TWO TERMS. William Jefferson "Bill" Clinton, a native son of Arkansas, became the 42nd President of the United States in 1993. He served two terms and focused much of his domestic priorities on creating a universal healthcare system, improving education, restricting handgun sales, and strengthening America's environmental regulations. When he left office, his approval rating was a lofty 65%.

25 FACTS

* Arkansas is called the Natural State.

* In 1880, General Douglas MacArthur was born in Little Rock.

* Arkansas is home to Bentonville. Here, Sam Walton founded his Wal-Mart stores.

* Arkansas is famous for the Ozark National Forest and its many hot springs.

* A person from Arkansas is called an Arkansan.

NATURAL RESOURCES. Arkansas ranks first in the world in its production of bromine, an element that's useful in making sanitizers, dyes, and flameproofing agents. Also, over 80% of our nation's bauxite comes from Arkansas. So, what's bauxite? It's the ore from which our aluminum is made.

Al Aluminum
Atomic Number: 13
Atomic Mass: 26.98

AR

GEOQUIZ

STATES	CAPITALS	BORDERS	TRIVIA
	My capital is MONTPELIER	I border Idaho, Wyoming, and Colorado.	The Great Salt Lake is in this state.
PAGE 49	PAGE 59	PAGE 58	PAGE 58

CALIFORNIA
CAPITAL: Sacramento
STATEHOOD: September 9, 1850

Population: 34,441,000	Area: 155,973 square miles
RANK: 1st	RANK: 3rd

Los Angeles San Diego San Jose

GOLD RUSH. James Marshall discovered gold at Sutter's Mill on January 24th, 1848. By the end of that year, news spread of this event and California's Gold Rush began. Soon thereafter, the region's population swelled and California was "rushed" into statehood.

Note: Those who came to search for gold in California were called '49ers because 1849 saw huge population growth in the area.

31 FACTS

* San Francisco Bay is considered to be the world's largest landlocked harbor.

* If California was its own country, it would have the world's 5th largest economy!

* Some of California's giant redwood trees are over 2,000 years old.

* Death Valley is considered the hottest and driest place in America.

* There are approximately 500,000 detectable seismic tremors in California each year!

A STICKY TREASURE. When the Portola Expedition passed through what is now California, Father Crespi wrote that a few members of their group saw "large marshes of a certain substance like pitch." Little did he know that the Rancho La Brea Tar Pits held the richest source of fossils in the world. So far, at least 60 species have been discovered in the tar springs, including saber-toothed cats, wolves, camels, bison, and mastodons.

CA

GEOQUIZ

STATES	CAPITALS	BORDERS	TRIVIA
	My capital is SANTA FE	I form Louisiana's EASTERN border.	Officially, this state was the first to join the Union.
PAGE 7	PAGE 42	PAGE 34	PAGE 15

COLORADO

CAPITAL: Denver

STATEHOOD: August 1, 1876

Population: 4,468,000	Area: 103,729 square miles
RANK: 24th	RANK: 8th

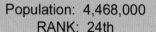

Denver Colorado Springs Aurora

CATTLEMEN. The National Western Stock Show is regarded as the "Super Bowl of Cattle Shows." When it began in 1904, only four types of cattle competed, and most of these came from Colorado and neighboring states. But now the yearly event has grown. Not only do 19 breeds of cattle come from around the world to compete, there are also events for bison, goats, llamas, swine, sheep, and dogs.

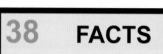

38 FACTS

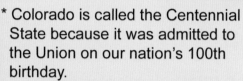

* Colorado is called the Centennial State because it was admitted to the Union on our nation's 100th birthday.

* More than 1/3 of Colorado's land is owned by the U.S. Federal Government.

* Colorado is home to the U.S. Air Force Academy.

* Colorado is split down the middle by the Rocky Mountains.

* Of all the states, Colorado has the highest average altitude.

PURPLE MOUNTAINS MAJESTY. In 1913, Katharine Lee Bates took a trip to Colorado Springs. While there, she visited Pike's Peak and said the following: "All the wonder of America seemed displayed there, with the sea-like expanse." Later, she penned the words to "America the Beautiful" and credited her visit to Colorado for the "purple mountains majesty" phrase.

CO

GEOQUIZ

STATES	CAPITALS	BORDERS	TRIVIA
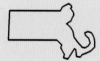	My capital is BOISE	Maryland forms my WESTERN border.	I am known as the BADGER State.
PAGE 30	PAGE 20	PAGE 15	PAGE 65

CONNECTICUT

CAPITAL: Hartford

STATEHOOD: January 9, 1788

Population: 3,317,000 RANK: 29th	Area: 4,845 square miles RANK: 48th

Bridgeport Hartford New Haven

THE CONSTITUTION STATE.
No, it wasn't the first state to ratify the Constitution; nor did it host the signing. So why is Connecticut called the Constitution State? Well, over 100 years before we gained our freedom from England, little Connecticut had adopted the Fundamental Orders. These laws are so similar to the American Constitution that the state has now become known as the CONSTITUTION State. So, now you know.

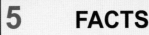

5 FACTS

* Connecticut's motto is: "He who transplanted still sustains."

* The oldest newspaper that's still being printed is *The Hartford Courant*. It had its debut in 1764.

* In 1954, the first nuclear powered submarine was built in Connecticut. It was named the USS Nautilus.

* Connecticut's Mary Kies was the first woman to receive a U.S. patent.

* Noah Webster, author of America's first dictionary, was from South Killingly.

FAMOUS FACES. Connecticut was home to many famous people: Ethan Allen (the Revolutionary War hero), John Brown (the abolitionist who sparked anti-slavery tensions), Elias Howe (a famous inventor), Charles Goodyear (another inventor), and Harriet Beecher Stowe (the author of Uncle Tom's Cabin). Each of these has helped to shape America.

CT

GEOQUIZ

STATES	CAPITALS	BORDERS	TRIVIA
	My capital is BISMARCK	I border New York and West Virginia.	I am home to the John F. Kennedy Space Center.
PAGE 53	PAGE 46	PAGE 51	PAGE 16

THE CIVIL WAR

Prior to the Civil War, the divisions between the North and South were largely fought in the Houses of Congress. However, by 1861, the Southern States went a step further by forming their own government, one that continued to support slavery, one of the most divisive issues between the two sides. This map shows the political landscape a few months prior to the war's beginning. You'll note that several states were neutral at the start; mostly because their populations were split regarding their sympathies. It wasn't until after four years of bloodshed and thousands of deaths that the war ended and the United States could once again be united.

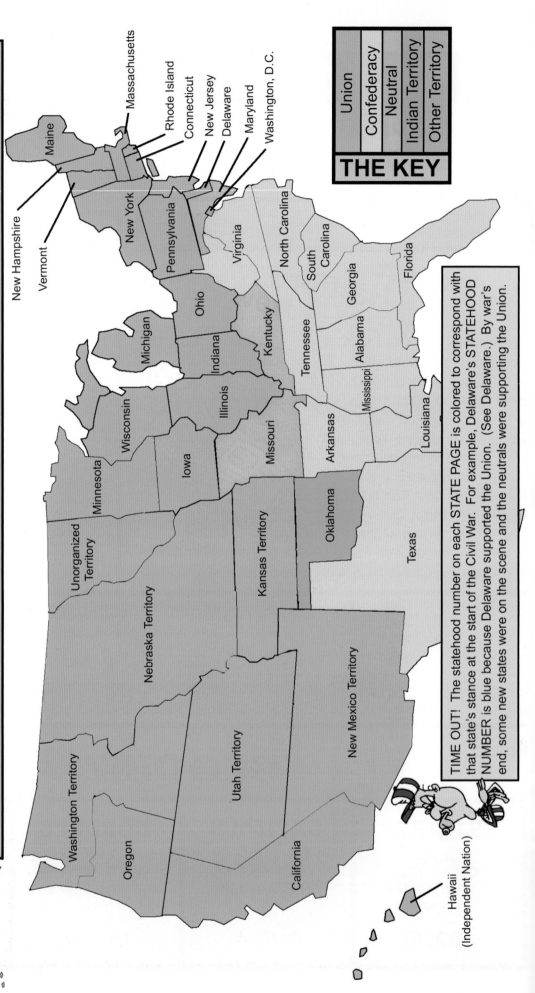

THE KEY

| Union |
| Confederacy |
| Neutral |
| Indian Territory |
| Other Territory |

TIME OUT! The statehood number on each STATE PAGE is colored to correspond with that state's stance at the start of the Civil War. For example, Delaware's STATEHOOD NUMBER is blue because Delaware supported the Union. (See Delaware.) By war's end, some new states were on the scene and the neutrals were supporting the Union.

Massachusetts
Rhode Island
Connecticut
New Jersey
Delaware
Maryland
Washington, D.C.

New Hampshire
Vermont

Maine
New York
Pennsylvania
Virginia
North Carolina
South Carolina
Georgia
Florida

Ohio
Michigan
Indiana
Kentucky
Tennessee
Alabama
Mississippi
Louisiana

Wisconsin
Illinois
Missouri
Arkansas

Minnesota
Iowa
Oklahoma
Texas

Unorganized Territory
Nebraska Territory
Kansas Territory
New Mexico Territory

Washington Territory
Oregon
Utah Territory
California

Alaska (Russia)

Hawaii (Independent Nation)

DELAWARE

CAPITAL: Dover
STATEHOOD: December 7, 1787

Population: 800,000
RANK: 46th

Area: 1,955 square miles
RANK: 49th

Wilmington Dover Newark

NUMBER 1. On December, 7th, 1787, the tiny state of Delaware had the distinction of leading our nation by becoming the first state to ratify the Constitution. That's right, the first state. Following its lead, the twelve other states existing at the time signed the document and the *United* States of America became official.

1 FACTS

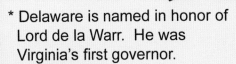
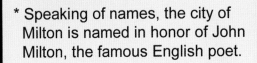

* Delaware is named in honor of Lord de la Warr. He was Virginia's first governor.

* Speaking of names, the city of Milton is named in honor of John Milton, the famous English poet.

* Losing his entire fortune in the fight against slavery, Delaware's Thomas Garret helped more than 2,000 slaves escape to freedom.

* Horseshoe crabs can be seen along the Delaware shores in May. These creatures can go nearly a year without any food!

NUMBER 2. OK, so Delaware doesn't have the second MOST land; that honor goes to Texas. But little Delaware does have the second LEAST amount of land. With a mere 1,955 square miles of space, only Rhode Island is smaller. Still, despite its small area, Delaware's people have done much for this nation.

NOTE: Alaska, the largest state, could hold 291 states the size of Delaware.

DE

GEOQUIZ

STATES	CAPITALS	BORDERS	TRIVIA
	My capital is SALT LAKE CITY	I border Mississippi, Arkansas, and Texas.	I am called the GREEN MOUNTAIN State.
PAGE 57	PAGE 58	PAGE 27	PAGE 59

16

FLORIDA

CAPITAL: Tallahassee
STATEHOOD: March 3, 1845

Population: 16,279,000	Area: 53,997 square miles
RANK: 4th	RANK: 26th

Jacksonville Miami Tampa

3-2-1-BLASTOFF! Cape Canaveral is home to the John F. Kennedy Space Center. Since July 1st, 1962, NASA has used this facility to launch heroic astronauts and various craft into space. From Project Mercury to the space shuttles, hundreds of missions have started in Florida.

NOTE: Before President Kennedy's death, NASA's Cape Canaveral location was simply called the Launch Operations Center.

27 FACTS

* Florida is called the Sunshine State.

* Saint Augustine is the oldest European settlement in North America.

* Of all the cities in America, Clearwater, Florida has the most lightning strikes each year.

* If you want to find the highest average temperature in the U.S., go to Key West.

* Florida is home to Walt Disney World, a famous amusement park.

THE ORANGE OASIS. Florida is the orange capital of the world. Nearly 75% of U.S. oranges come from this state, and Florida produces almost 40% of the WORLD's orange juice supply! Surprisingly, however, the orange isn't native to Florida. In 1493, Christopher Columbus brought orange seeds to the Carolinas. Then, in 1513, explorer Ponce De Leon brought them to Florida.

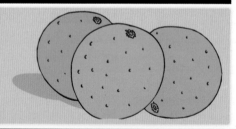

FL

GEOQUIZ

STATES	CAPITALS	BORDERS	TRIVIA
	My capital is JUNEAU	I border Florida and Mississippi.	Baltimore is the largest city in this state.
PAGE 10	PAGE 7	PAGE 6	PAGE 29

GEORGIA

CAPITAL: Atlanta
STATEHOOD: January 2, 1788

Population: 8,413,000	Area: 57,198 square miles
RANK: 9th	RANK: 21st

Atlanta   Augusta   Columbus

THE PEACH STATE. Georgia is quite famous for the quality and quantity of peaches it grows, but did you know the peach isn't native to Georgia? The fruit was first cultivated in China thousands of years ago. Later, it made its way along trading routes to Persia and Europe. Then, during the 16th and 17th centuries, Spanish ships carried the tasty fruit to the shores of America.

4 FACTS

* Georgia is named for England's King George II.

* Jimmy Carter is from Georgia. He was the 39th President of the United States.

* Georgia has more land than any other state east of the Mississippi River.

* The famous pirate Edward Teach made a home on an island that's now part of Georgia. Who's Teach? He's better known as "Blackbeard."

* Georgia is called the Peach State and the Cracker State.

PEANUTS. Loved throughout the world, the peanut has become an important product for Georgia, where almost 40% of America's peanuts are grown. But like the peach, it isn't native to North America. Evidence suggests it originated in South America. So, how did it get to Georgia? Well, from South America, the Portuguese took the peanut to Africa, where it grew in popularity. From there, it was brought back across the Atlantic Ocean to America.

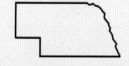

GA

GEOQUIZ

STATES	CAPITALS	BORDERS	TRIVIA
	My capital is ALBANY	I border Washington and California.	I am called the CONSTITUTION State.
PAGE 37	PAGE 43	PAGE 49	PAGE 13

HAWAII

CAPITAL: Honolulu
STATEHOOD: August 21, 1959

Population: 1,342,000	Area: 6,423 square miles
RANK: 40th	RANK: 47th

Honolulu   Hilo   Kailua

DECEMBER 7th. Hawaii is home to Pearl Harbor. During the morning hours of December 7th, 1941, combat planes from the Japanese fleet attacked our fleet while it was stationed there. Within ten minutes, five battleships were sunk or sinking, many American airplanes were destroyed, and over 2,400 Americans were dead. Sadly, what started as a peaceful Sunday morning turned into a call to arms and America's entry into the Second World War.

50 FACTS

* At one time, Hawaii was ruled by kings and queens. In fact, Hawaii's Iolani palace is the only royal palace in the U.S.

* Eight main islands help to form the state of Hawaii.

* Wow. Hawaii, not Florida, is the southernmost state.

* Unlike most states, the wind usually blows from east to west in Hawaii.

* Did you know that 1/3 of the world's pineapple supply comes from Hawaii?

THE LAST PIECE? In 1959, Hawaii became the last state to enter the Union. From thirteen to fifty, the United States has grown into one of the strongest nations in the world, and although there is currently no foreseeable 51st piece on the horizon, many are pushing to make Washington, D.C. a state. Another contender is Puerto Rico, an island territory off the coast of Florida. But, for now, the Aloha State maintains its status as the final piece to the American puzzle.

HI

GEOQUIZ

STATES	CAPITALS	BORDERS	TRIVIA
	CONGRATULATIONS! You have completed the CAPITALS challenge.	I border Maryland and North Carolina.	The Salem Witchcraft Trials took place in this state.
PAGE 13		PAGE 61	PAGE 30

STATEHOOD

19

ORDER OF ADMISSION. Find your state on the list below. Are you from Hawaii? If so, your state was the 50th to join the Union. Which state was first? That's right, Delaware was our first state. Now find North Dakota and South Dakota. What numbers are they? They BOTH are 39th OR 40th! Do you know why? Well, when these two became states, not only were they admitted on the same date, they were admitted at the exact same time; so they share the two spots.

THE THIRTEEN COLONIES

1. DELAWARE
2. PENNSYLVANIA
3. NEW JERSEY
4. GEORGIA
5. CONNECTICUT
6. MASSACHUSETTS
7. MARYLAND
8. SOUTH CAROLINA
9. NEW HAMPSHIRE
10. VIRGINIA
11. NEW YORK
12. NORTH CAROLINA
13. RHODE ISLAND
14. Vermont
15. Kentucky
16. Tennessee
17. Ohio
18. Louisiana
19. Indiana
20. Mississippi
21. Illinois
22. Alabama
23. Maine
24. Missouri
25. Arkansas
26. Michigan
27. Florida
28. Texas
29. Iowa
30. Wisconsin
31. California
32. Minnesota
33. Oregon
34. Kansas
35. West Virginia
36. Nevada
37. Nebraska
38. Colorado
39. North Dakota OR South Dakota
40. North Dakota OR South Dakota
41. Montana
42. Washington
43. Idaho
44. Wyoming
45. Utah
46. Oklahoma
47. New Mexico
48. Arizona
49. Alaska
50. Hawaii

20

IDAHO

CAPITAL: Boise
STATEHOOD: July 3, 1890

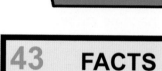

Population: 1,480,000 RANK: 39th	Area: 82,751 square miles RANK: 11th

Boise Nampa Idaho Falls

SCENIC WONDERLAND. Idaho is an outdoor adventure. Alpine lakes, mountain peaks, canyons, and waterfalls are just some of the splendor the state has to offer. Also, because of the variety of landscapes, you can visit rolling hills, hot springs, and even high country deserts and sand dunes! And the wildlife? It's abundant. Without a doubt, Idaho offers plenty to those who enjoy the outdoors.

43 FACTS

* Idaho is known as the Gem State because of the many precious stones that can be found there.

* Like most western states, Idaho had its gold and silver rushes. Today, a number of "ghost" towns remain. They include: Silver City, Yankee Fork, and Gold Dredge.

* The world's largest man-made geyser can be found in Soda Springs.

* Beware! In Idaho, it's against the law for one citizen to give another a box of candy weighing more than 50 pounds!

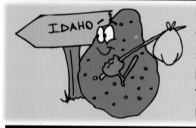

IDAHO AND THE POTATO. When many think of Idaho, they think of the potato, because over 30% of American potatoes come from the state. But few know the potato isn't native to Idaho. Many scientists believe the spud had its beginnings in South America and was brought to North America long before Columbus arrived; however, it wasn't until 1836 that it found a home in Idaho!

GEOQUIZ

STATES	CAPITALS	BORDERS	TRIVIA
	My capital is HONOLULU	I am completely surrounded by the PACIFIC OCEAN.	I border EIGHT states, but I'm not Tennessee.
PAGE 51	PAGE 18	PAGE 18	PAGE 35

ILLINOIS

CAPITAL: Springfield

STATEHOOD: December 3, 1818

Population: 12,266,000 RANK: 6th	Area: 55,593 square miles RANK: 24th

Chicago Aurora Rockford

THE GIPPER. Illinois is the birthplace of Ronald Wilson Reagan, the 40th President of the United States. Born in Tampico, Reagan moved to California, where he became an actor. Later, he stepped onto the political stage and was elected California's governor. President Reagan served two terms in the White House and is credited with winning the Cold War.

21 FACTS

* In 1871, the Great Chicago Fire killed about 200 people, destroyed 17,500 buildings, and left nearly 90,000 people homeless.

* Illinois was the first state to ratify the 13th Amendment to the Constitution. This law abolished slavery.

* The world's first skyscraper was built in Chicago, not New York.

* If you're looking for a good book, come to Chicago. Its public library has over two million books, making it one of the world's largest.

A BUSY, BUSY PLACE. Chicago's O'Hare International Airport is the busiest airport in the world. Even when you consider its large number of connections to multiple locations throughout the world, it's still hard to imagine that over 190,000 travelers pass through its terminals on a normal day.

IL

GEOQUIZ

STATES	CAPITALS	BORDERS	TRIVIA
	My capital is DENVER	I form Georgia's SOUTHERN border.	This state has the most land area, by far.
PAGE 17	PAGE 12	PAGE 16	PAGE 7

INDIANA
CAPITAL: Indianapolis
STATEHOOD: December 11, 1816

Population: 6,215,000
RANK: 15th

Area: 35,870 square miles
RANK: 38th

Indianapolis Fort Wayne Evansville

ONE BATTLE. Corydon was the site of Indiana's only Civil War battle. In 1863, Confederate General John Hunt Morgan led 2,400 of his soldiers on a daring raid through the Northern state. Shortly after entering Indiana, the Rebels met Harrison County's small force of 450 men. After a few volleys, Morgan accepted their surrender. He met no further resistance until after he entered Ohio.

19 FACTS

* Indiana is called the Hoosier State.

* In addition to being the site of Indiana's only Civil War battle, Corydon also served as the state's first capital.

* The first Europeans to settle in what is now Indiana were not the English. They were French.

* Southern Indiana holds some of the richest deposits of limestone in the world! New York's Empire State Building, the U.S. Treasury, and fourteen state capitol buildings are built from Indiana's treasure.

THE INDIANAPOLIS 500. In 1911, the first long-distance auto race was held in the city of Indianapolis. Since then, this yearly event has attracted more fans, faster cars, and more money for the winner. The winner of the first race averaged 75 miles per hour and received a $14,000 prize. Today, speeds average around 167 miles per hour and the winner receives more than 1.2 million dollars.

IN

GEOQUIZ

STATES	CAPITALS	BORDERS	TRIVIA
	My capital is ATLANTA	I border Texas and Kansas.	At the beginning of the Civil War, this state was part of Virginia.
PAGE 20	PAGE 17	PAGE 48	PAGE 64

IOWA

CAPITAL: Des Moines
STATEHOOD: December 28, 1846

| Population: 2,941,000 | Area: 55,875 square miles |
| RANK: 30th | RANK: 23rd |

Des Moines   Cedar Rapids   Davenport

CORN. There are believed to be over 3,500 uses for corn. From aspirin to diapers, from food to automobile fuel, it seems new ways of using this important crop are being discovered every day.

NOTE: Of the nearly 10 billion bushels of corn grown yearly in the U.S., roughly 57% is fed to livestock, 19% is exported to other countries, and 12% is used in ethanol fuel. America's five biggest customers for corn are: Japan, Mexico, Taiwan, South Korea, and Egypt.

29 FACTS

* Herbert Hoover, the 31st President of the United States, was from Iowa. He was the first president to be born west of the Mississippi River.

* John Wayne, the famous actor, was born in Winterset. Many remember him as "The Duke."

* Glenn Miller, orchestra leader and trombonist, was born in Clarinda.

* The Mississippi River forms Iowa's eastern border and the Missouri River forms its western border.

THE BIG BREADBASKET. It has been estimated that each farmer in Iowa produces enough food to feed 279 people. Now that's what I call productive! Corn, soybeans, and hogs are just some of the sources of nutrition that come from the Hawkeye State. So, the next time you visit the grocery store, remember that a small part of Iowa may be in your buggy.

IA

GEOQUIZ

STATES	CAPITALS	BORDERS	TRIVIA
	My capital is NASHVILLE	I border Missouri and West Virginia.	I share my name with the longest river in the United States.
PAGE 64	PAGE 56	PAGE 26	PAGE 34

KANSAS

CAPITAL: Topeka
STATEHOOD: January 29, 1861

Population: 2,761,000 RANK: 32nd	Area: 81,823 square miles RANK: 13th

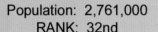

Wichita Overland Park Kansas City

WATCH OUT! Tornadoes are storms with rapidly rotating winds that form funnel clouds. Unfortunately, many of these touch the ground, causing much damage with their nearly 300 mile per hour winds. As you may recall in the movie "The Wizard of Oz," a Kansas girl by the name of Dorothy was even whisked away by one. But is Kansas the most active tornado state? No, it isn't! On average, three other states receive more. And in relation to land size, Kansas ranks a distant fifth.

34 FACTS

* Dodge City is proclaimed to be the windiest city in America.

* The geographic center of the 48 contiguous states is in Kansas.

* The first woman mayor in the U.S. was from Kansas. In 1887, Susan Salter was elected to office in Argonia.

* Kansas is important to U.S. land surveyors. When they're outside checking the positions of properties, they're really checking their positions in relation to Kansas' Meades Ranch, our nation's benchmark.

AMELIA EARHART. The most famous woman in aviation history is from Kansas. In 1932, Amelia Earhart became the first woman (and only the second person) to fly solo across the Atlantic Ocean. Then, in 1935, she became the first person to fly solo from Hawaii to California. However, her career was cut short in 1937 when she perished in the Pacific Ocean after failing to find a small island that was to serve as her landing site.

KS

GEOQUIZ

STATES	CAPITALS	BORDERS	TRIVIA
PAGE 39	My capital is BOSTON PAGE 30	I border Canada and Utah. PAGE 20	The Wright Brothers successfully flew their first airplane in this state. PAGE 45

ABBREVIATIONS

25

AL	Alabama
AK	Alaska
AZ	Arizona
AR	Arkansas
CA	California
CO	Colorado
CT	Connecticut
DE	Delaware
FL	Florida
GA	Georgia
HI	Hawaii
ID	Idaho
IL	Illinois
IN	Indiana
IA	Iowa
KS	Kansas
KY	Kentucky
LA	Louisiana
ME	Maine
MD	Maryland
MA	Massachusetts
MI	Michigan
MN	Minnesota
MS	Mississippi
MO	Missouri

MT	Montana
NE	Nebraska
NV	Nevada
NH	New Hampshire
NJ	New Jersey
NM	New Mexico
NY	New York
NC	North Carolina
ND	North Dakota
OH	Ohio
OK	Oklahoma
OR	Oregon
PA	Pennsylvania
RI	Rhode Island
SC	South Carolina
SD	South Dakota
TN	Tennessee
TX	Texas
UT	Utah
VT	Vermont
VA	Virginia
WA	Washington
WV	West Virginia
WI	Wisconsin
WY	Wyoming

ABBREVIATIONS. Have you ever addressed an envelope? If so, you may have used some of the abbreviations listed above. They are true time savers that the U.S. Postal Service developed.

NOTE: The abbreviation for Washington, D.C. is simply *DC*.

KENTUCKY

CAPITAL: Frankfort
STATEHOOD: June 1, 1792

Population: 4,098,000 RANK: 25th	Area: 39,732 square miles RANK: 36th

Louisville Lexington Owensboro

ABRAHAM LINCOLN

FAMOUS KENTUCKIAN. Abraham Lincoln was born in Kentucky in 1809. After moving with his family to Illinois, the young man took it upon himself to grow in knowledge. Working on farms, splitting rails, and tending to a store were only some of the duties Lincoln performed. However, his passion soon turned to politics, where he was able to represent the Republican Party, win the 1860 Presidential Election, and lead America through the most trying period of its history, the Civil War.

15 FACTS

* Jefferson Davis was from Kentucky. He served as the Confederate president during the Civil War.

* During the War of 1812, over half of all the Americans killed were from Kentucky, the Bluegrass State.

* Kentucky is home to Fort Knox. Much of the nation's gold is held here.

* More than 100 Kentuckians have been governors of OTHER states!

* The Kentucky Derby is the oldest yearly horse race in the country.

NATURAL WONDER. Mammoth Cave is true to its name. It's a whopper! Even with over 365 miles of charted passageways, it's still believed that there are hundreds of miles left to be discovered. Nearly two million people visit the huge cavern each year to see "rooms" large enough to hold office buildings, underground rivers, and creatures that can seldom be seen anywhere else in the world.

KY

GEOQUIZ

STATES	CAPITALS	BORDERS	TRIVIA
CONGRATULATIONS! You have completed the STATES challenge.	My capital is AUSTIN	New Hampshire forms my EASTERN border.	I am home to Detroit, Grand Rapids, and Warren.
	PAGE 57	PAGE 59	PAGE 32

LOUISIANA

CAPITAL: Baton Rouge
STATEHOOD: April 30, 1812

Population: 4,535,000	Area: 43,566 square miles
RANK: 23rd	RANK: 33rd

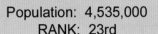
New Orleans Baton Rouge Shreveport

THEY WOULD NOT BOW. A large number of Cajuns live in Louisiana, but do you know what makes these people special? Why, they're the descendants of the Acadians who were driven out of Canada during the 1700s. OK, and who were the Acadians? The Acadians were the first FRENCH settlers in what are now the Canadian provinces of Nova Scotia, New Brunswick, and Prince Edward Island. They were forced from Canada when they refused to pledge allegiance to the King of *England*.

18 FACTS

* Louisiana was named in honor of France's King Louis XIV.

* During the Civil War, twenty major battles took place in Louisiana during a two-year span.

* The Mississippi River meets the Gulf of Mexico in Louisiana.

* The word "bayou" is French. It signifies a slow-moving river.

* Jazz, a form of music, had its birth in Louisiana. In the 1920s and 1930s, it reached its height of popularity.

FAT TUESDAY. What would you do the day before forty days of fasting was to begin? Well, they throw a party in New Orleans! Mardi Gras (meaning "Fat Tuesday" in French) is a festival that has become a yearly event in Louisiana. Coming the day before the Christian observance of Lent, the celebration is still growing in popularity, even after 300 years.

LA

GEOQUIZ

STATES	CAPITALS	BORDERS	TRIVIA
	My capital is SACRAMENTO	I border Colorado and Iowa.	I am called the CENTENNIAL State.
PAGE 65	PAGE 11	PAGE 37	PAGE 12

MAINE

CAPITAL: Augusta
STATEHOOD: March 15, 1820

Population: 1,285,000	Area: 30,865 square miles
RANK: 41st	RANK: 39th

Portland   Lewiston   Bangor

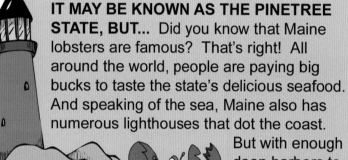

IT MAY BE KNOWN AS THE PINETREE STATE, BUT... Did you know that Maine lobsters are famous? That's right! All around the world, people are paying big bucks to taste the state's delicious seafood. And speaking of the sea, Maine also has numerous lighthouses that dot the coast. But with enough deep harbors to handle all the navies of the world, they are necessary.

23   FACTS

* Eastport is America's easternmost city. It's said to be the first place in the U.S. to see the morning sun.

* Maine's Acadia National Park is the second most visited national park in America.

* Poet Henry Wadsworth Longfellow was from Maine.

* In 1623, America's first sawmill was built near York, Maine.

* After the War of 1812, Eastport remained in British hands. Their rule didn't end until 1818.

BEAUTIFUL LAND. Nearly 90% of America's toothpicks come from Maine's timber, and the state's production of blueberries is second to none. In fact, about 99% of all our blueberries come from Maine! That's right, 99%! And then there's the snow. With its alpine mountains, the state is a great place for those who love the outdoors.

ME

GEOQUIZ

STATES	CAPITALS	BORDERS	TRIVIA
	My capital is TOPEKA	I border Alabama and South Carolina.	Mount Rushmore is in this state.
PAGE 27	PAGE 24	PAGE 17	PAGE 54

MARYLAND

CAPITAL: Annapolis
STATEHOOD: April 28, 1788

Population: 5,467,000	Area: 9,755 square miles
RANK: 19th	RANK: 42nd

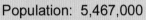
Baltimore Gaithersburg Rockville

7 FACTS

* Did you know that Maryland gave up some of its land to help form Washington, D.C.? Virginia was the only other state to lend a hand.

* Clara Barton was the founder of the American Red Cross. At one time, her home in Glen Echo served as the organization's headquarters.

* Other famous Marylanders include: Vice President Spiro Agnew, author Upton Sinclair, baseball great Babe Ruth, and abolitionists Harriet Tubman and Frederick Douglas.

OH SAY, CAN YOU SEE?

During the War of 1812, Washington, D.C. was captured by the British, and the city of Baltimore was next. Through the Maryland harbor, British warships made their approach, but Fort McHenry stood in their way. From the deck of a ship, Francis Scott Key, a patriot, watched the fort being bombarded. Through the night, he stood, and when he saw America's flag still waving in the morning, he penned the words to our national anthem.

ANNAPOLIS. Once called the Athens of America, the city of Annapolis is a national treasure: the Maryland city once served as our nation's capital; since 1845 it has served as the home of the U.S. Naval Academy; four signers of the Declaration of Independence lived there; it boasts more surviving colonial buildings than any other city; and it was where the Treaty of Paris was ratified in 1784 to end the Revolutionary War.

MD

GEOQUIZ

STATES	CAPITALS	BORDERS	TRIVIA
	My capital is TRENTON	I border Montana and Colorado.	I am called the CORNHUSKER State.
PAGE 26	PAGE 41	PAGE 66	PAGE 37

30

MASSACHUSETTS

CAPITAL: Boston
STATEHOOD: February 6, 1788

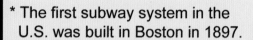
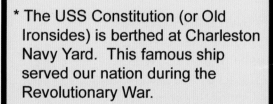

Population: 6,310,000 RANK: 13th	Area: 7,838 square miles RANK: 45th

Boston Worcester Springfield

THE PILGRIMS. On December 21st, 1620, a group of English Puritans came to America aboard the Mayflower. Their intent was to escape religious persecution, create a new settlement, and practice religion the way they felt was right. The famous place where they landed is known as Plymouth Rock.

THANKSGIVING

6 FACTS

* The first subway system in the U.S. was built in Boston in 1897.

* The USS Constitution (or Old Ironsides) is berthed at Charleston Navy Yard. This famous ship served our nation during the Revolutionary War.

* The Boston Tea Party took place in Massachusetts shortly before the Revolutionary War began.

* In 1692, the infamous Salem Witchcraft Trials led to the deaths of twenty citizens.

HEROES OF THE REVOLUTION. Minutemen played a vital role in the American Revolution, especially in Massachusetts. Armed, mobile, and always ready for action, these brave men were usually the first to arrive for battle.

MA

GEOQUIZ

STATES	CAPITALS	BORDERS	TRIVIA
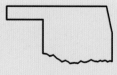	My capital is SALEM	I border Iowa and Arkansas.	I am called the BEAVER State.
PAGE 48	PAGE 49	PAGE 35	PAGE 49

THE PRESIDENTS

NAME	STATE OF BIRTH	TERM OF OFFICE
1. George Washington	Virginia	1789 - 1797
2. John Adams	Massachusetts	1797 - 1801
3. Thomas Jefferson	Virginia	1801 - 1809
4. James Madison	Virginia	1809 - 1817
5. James Monroe	Virginia	1817 - 1825
6. John Quincy Adams	Massachusetts	1825 - 1829
7. Andrew Jackson	South Carolina	1829 - 1837
8. Martin Van Buren	New York	1837 - 1841
9. William Henry Harrison	Virginia	1841
10. John Tyler	Virginia	1841 - 1845
11. James Polk	North Carolina	1845 - 1849
12. Zachary Taylor	Virginia	1849 - 1850
13. Millard Fillmore	New York	1850 - 1853
14. Franklin Pierce	New Hampshire	1853 - 1857
15. James Buchanan	Pennsylvania	1857 - 1861
16. Abraham Lincoln	Kentucky	1861 - 1865
17. Andrew Johnson	North Carolina	1865 - 1869
18. Ulysses S. Grant	Ohio	1869 - 1877
19. Rutherford B. Hayes	Ohio	1877 - 1881
20. James A. Garfield	Ohio	1881
21. Chester A. Arthur	Vermont	1881 - 1885
22. Grover Cleveland	New Jersey	1885 - 1889
23. Benjamin Harrison	Ohio	1889 - 1893
24. Grover Cleveland	New Jersey	1893 - 1897
25. William McKinley	Ohio	1897 - 1901
26. Theodore Roosevelt	New York	1901 - 1909
27. William H. Taft	Ohio	1909 - 1913
28. Woodrow Wilson	Virginia	1913 - 1921
29. Warren Harding	Ohio	1921 - 1923
30. Calvin Coolidge	Vermont	1923 - 1929
31. Herbert Hoover	Iowa	1929 - 1933
32. Franklin D. Roosevelt	New York	1933 - 1945
33. Harry S. Truman	Missouri	1945 - 1953
34. Dwight D. Eisenhower	Texas	1953 - 1961
35. John F. Kennedy	Massachusetts	1961 - 1963
36. Lyndon B. Johnson	Texas	1963 - 1969
37. Richard Nixon	California	1969 - 1974
38. Gerald R. Ford	Nebraska	1974 - 1977
39. Jimmy Carter	Georgia	1977 - 1981
40. Ronald Reagan	Illinois	1981 - 1989
41. George Herbert Walker Bush	Massachusetts	1989 - 1993
42. Willam Jefferson Clinton	Arkansas	1993 - 2001
43. George W. Bush	Connecticut	2001 -

CAN YOU ANSWER THESE?
1. Which state can boast having the most presidents born in it?
2. Which president served the most time in office?
3. How many different men have been president?

Answers: 1) Virginia 2) Franklin Roosevelt 3) 42 men! (Grover Cleveland is listed twice.)

MICHIGAN

CAPITAL: Lansing
STATEHOOD: January 26, 1837

Population: 9,763,000
RANK: 8th

Area: 56,809 square miles
RANK: 22nd

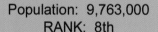
Detroit Grand Rapids Warren

THE WOLVERINE STATE.
Michigan is the Wolverine State, but what exactly is a wolverine? Well, the wolverine is a member of Mustelidae family (animals such as skunks, otters, and weasels). Though small in 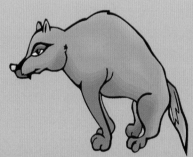 size, the powerfully-built animal is suited for winter survival and is fearless. As a matter of fact, the wolverine won't hesitate to attack sheep, deer, or even small bears! Sadly, the wolverine is on the endangered species list and can no longer be found in Michigan.

26 FACTS

* The University of Michigan was the first university to be established in any state.

* Gerald R. Ford, the 38th President of the United States, was raised in Grand Rapids.

* The Detroit Zoo was the first zoo to offer cageless exhibits.

* Boats, boats, and more boats. Michigan has more boats registered in it than any other state.

* The Detroit-Windsor tunnel was the first tunnel to connect two countries.

CAR CAPITAL OF THE WORLD. Yes, the city of Detroit and the surrounding area have helped turn Michigan into the largest manufacturer of cars. The Ford Motor Company, General Motors, and DaimlerChrysler call Michigan their home. Together, these three have placed millions of vehicles on the road.

MI

GEOQUIZ

STATES	CAPITALS	BORDERS	TRIVIA
	My capital is HARTFORD	I border Maryland, Virginia, and Kentucky.	President Jimmy Carter was born in this southern state.
PAGE 21	PAGE 13	PAGE 64	PAGE 17

MINNESOTA
CAPITAL: Saint Paul
STATEHOOD: May 11, 1858

Population: 5,005,000	Area: 79,617 square miles
RANK: 21st	RANK: 14th

Minneapolis Saint Paul Rochester

FISHING, ANYONE? With more than 90,000 miles of shoreline, Minnesota has more than California, Florida, and Hawaii combined. Couple that with the excellent fishing, and it's no wonder the state boasts having one recreational boat for every six of its citizens. But beware of meeting someone at Mud Lake, Rice Lake, or Long Lake. With over 10,000 bodies of water, these common names have been used over 100 times each!

32 FACTS

* Minnesota is known as the Land of 10,000 Lakes, but that is a low estimate.

* Minnesota is home to the Mayo Clinic. This teaching facility is known throughout the world for its expertise in the medical field.

* America's first bone marrow transplant took place in Minnesota.

* Have you ever eaten a Snickers, 3 Musketeers, or Milky Way bar? Frank C. Mars, the inventor of these tasty treats, was from Minnesota.

DID THE VIKINGS REACH AMERICA BEFORE COLUMBUS? An archeological site in Minnesota suggests that they might have. In 1898, the Kensington Runestone was discovered near Alexandria, Minnesota. Its carvings tell the journey of a band of Vikings that reached North America in 1362, over 100 years before Columbus. Also, evidence in eastern Canada suggests that Leif Eirikson entered the Gulf of Saint Lawrence.

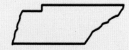

GEOQUIZ

STATES	CAPITALS	BORDERS	TRIVIA
	My capital is TALLAHASSEE	I border Idaho and North Dakota.	I am called the VOLUNTEER State.
PAGE 56	PAGE 16	PAGE 36	PAGE 56

MISSISSIPPI

CAPITAL: Jackson
STATEHOOD: December 10, 1817

Population: 2,908,000
RANK: 31st

Area: 46,614 square miles
RANK: 31st

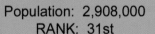 Jackson  Gulfport Biloxi

THE KING. Elvis Presley, also known as the King of Rock and Roll, was born in Tupelo, Mississippi on January 8th, 1935. For more than two decades, the singer set and broke many records for both record sales and concert attendance. Some of his music includes: "Love Me Tender," "Jailhouse Rock," and "Kentucky Rain." Elvis passed away in 1977, but millions of fans from around the world continue to buy his music.

20 FACTS

* In 1902, President Theodore Roosevelt refused to shoot a captured bear while he was visiting Mississippi. His kind act led to the creation of the cuddly "Teddy" bear, a bedroom favorite.

* 59,000 of the 78,000 Mississippians who fought in the Civil War were either wounded or killed in action.

* Captain Isaac Ross was from Mississippi. Who is he? In 1834, Captain Ross freed his slaves and made arrangements to send them to Africa. There, they founded the country of Liberia.

OLD MAN RIVER. Mississippi shares its name with America's longest river, the Mississippi River. Forming much of the state's western border, the mighty river has played an important role in the development of the country. In the 1800s, riverboats transported people and goods along the river, turning many towns into lively cities with strong economies. Mark Twain's "The Adventures of Huckleberry Finn" captures this spirit.

MS

GEOQUIZ

STATES	CAPITALS	BORDERS	TRIVIA
	My capital is HARRISBURG	I border Michigan and Minnesota.	I am called the PALMETTO State.
PAGE 29	PAGE 51	PAGE 65	PAGE 53

MISSOURI

CAPITAL: Jefferson City
STATEHOOD: August 10, 1821

Population: 5,718,000	Area: 68,898 square miles
RANK: 17th	RANK: 18th

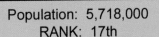

Kansas City Saint Louis Springfield

PENNSYLVANIA OF THE WEST?

Missouri is called the "Show Me State," but some still refer to it as the "Pennsylvania of the West." Why? Well, while Missouri's economy developed with its rise in population, many noticed the similarities between its growth and that of Pennsylvania. Mining was of great importance and, likewise, manufacturing within the state was on the rise.

24 FACTS

* Missouri, like Tennessee, borders eight states. No other states border as many.

* President Harry S. Truman was born in Lamar. He was president at the close of the Second World War.

* Saint Louis is home to the famous Gateway Arch. During the 1960s, this monument was built to honor the spirit of the early pioneers.

* Saint Louis. In 1912, John Berry made the first successful parachute jump from a moving airplane.

THE GROUND SHOOK. The most powerful earthquake to shake America didn't occur in California; it was in New Madrid, Missouri. At two o'clock in the morning on December 16th, 1811, the quake started. Huge cracks split the ground; the waters of the Mississippi River rose and fell so forcefully that giant waves swept upstream to Louisville, Kentucky; and church bells were made to ring in Boston, Massachusetts, which was over 1,000 miles away!

MO

GEOQUIZ

STATES	CAPITALS	BORDERS	TRIVIA
	My capital is ANNAPOLIS	I border Utah and Kansas.	I am home to Philadelphia and Pittsburgh.
PAGE 40	PAGE 29	PAGE 12	PAGE 51

MONTANA

CAPITAL: Helena
STATEHOOD: November 8, 1889

Population: 1,006,000   Area: 145,556 square miles
RANK: 44th   RANK: 4th

Billings Missoula Great Falls

THE TREASURE STATE.
Montana is home to some of America's richest deposits of rare minerals. When gold was discovered in 1862, many settlers came to the area, hoping to strike it rich. In time, they discovered copper, silver, sapphires, opals, and platinum. Today, many of the areas where mining occurred have become ghost towns, but Montana's resources still touch all our lives.

41 FACTS

* Montana has more species of mammals than any other state.

* If you're looking for deer, elk, or antelope, you've come to the right place. The state is teeming with them.

* Yellowstone National Park was our country's first national park. The park covers areas of Montana, Wyoming, and Idaho.

* Lots of land and few people. With only six people per square mile, Montana offers plenty of elbow room.

YELLOW HAIR. Montana is home to the Little Bighorn Battlefield. Here, in 1876, Lt. Colonel George Custer and the Seventh Cavalry fell in battle to a group of Sioux and Cheyenne Indians that left their reservations, outraged by the continued intrusions of gold seekers into their sacred lands in the Black Hills. In the end, the Union Cavalry lost over 260 men and the Indian alliance lost nearly 200.

MT

GEOQUIZ

STATES	CAPITALS	BORDERS	TRIVIA
	My capital is CONCORD	Connecticut forms my western border.	I am called the OCEAN State.
PAGE 34	PAGE 40	PAGE 52	PAGE 52

NEBRASKA

CAPITAL: Lincoln
STATEHOOD: March 1, 1867

Population: 1,761,000
RANK: 38th

Area: 75,898 square miles
RANK: 15th

Omaha   Lincoln   Bellevue

MOO. Although Nebraska ranks 38th in population, its cattle industry is one of the top in the nation. Here are a few facts: Nebraska ranks 1st in its number of live animal and beef exports; 2nd in the amount of revenues it receives from the sales of cattle and calves; and 3rd in its total number of cattle. With an estimated 6.35 MILLION head, Nebraska holds almost 7% of our nation's herd!

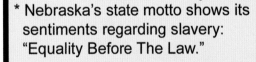

37   FACTS

* Nebraska's state motto shows its sentiments regarding slavery: "Equality Before The Law."

* Most states have two houses of legislature: a house and a senate. However, Nebraska only has one.

* Weeping Water is home to the nation's largest limestone deposit.

* During World War II, over 40% of our nation's ammunition was made in Hastings, Nebraska.

* President Gerald R. Ford was born in Nebraska.

THE CORNHUSKER STATE. As its nickname implies, Nebraska is a large producer of corn, but this wasn't always the case. At one time, Nebraska was called the "Great American Desert." Thankfully, those days are gone and the state has been transformed into a farmer's paradise through the use of progressive farming techniques and irrigation. In fact, with over 80,000 wells to draw water from, Nebraska has become the 3rd largest corn-producing state.

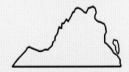
NE

GEOQUIZ

STATES	CAPITALS	BORDERS	TRIVIA
	My capital is PROVIDENCE	I border Oregon, Nevada, and Arizona.	CONGRATULATIONS! You have completed the TRIVIA challenge.
PAGE 61	PAGE 52	PAGE 11	

PAGE 61 — PAGE 52 — PAGE 11

POPULATION RANKINGS

LOOKING AT THE NUMBERS. Look at the chart below. Can you find your state? All 50 states have been listed in order with the most populous states coming first. California leads the way with the most people; Texas is second; and New York is holding on to the third slot. On the other end of the chart, you'll find the states with the fewest people. Wyoming (ranked 50th) has the least number of people living in it; Vermont is 49th; and North Dakota is 48th.

1. California
2. Texas
3. New York
4. Florida
5. Pennsylvania
6. Illinois
7. Ohio
8. Michigan
9. Georgia
10. New Jersey
11. North Carolina
12. Virginia
13. Massachusetts
14. Washington
15. Indiana
16. Tennessee
17. Missouri
18. Wisconsin
19. Maryland
20. Arizona
21. Minnesota
22. Alabama
23. Louisiana
24. Colorado
25. Kentucky
26. South Carolina
27. Oregon
28. Oklahoma
29. Connecticut
30. Iowa
31. Mississippi
32. Kansas
33. Arkansas
34. Utah
35. Nevada
36. New Mexico
37. West Virginia
38. Nebraska
39. Idaho
40. Hawaii
41. Maine
42. New Hampshire
43. Rhode Island
44. Montana
45. South Dakota
46. Delaware
47. Alaska
48. North Dakota
49. Vermont
50. Wyoming

NEVADA

CAPITAL: Carson City
STATEHOOD: October 31, 1864

Population: 2,070,000   Area: 109,806 square miles
RANK: 35th   RANK: 7th

Las Vegas Henderson Reno

CHANGE OF CAREER.
Shortly after the Civil War began, a riverboat pilot by the name of Samuel Clemens realized that it wouldn't be profitable to work along the Mississippi River anymore. So, he packed his bags, moved to Nevada, and

became a silver miner. However, he failed in the mines and settled for becoming a writer for a local newspaper, the *Daily Territorial Enterprise*. As time would prove, his career change uncovered a literary lode. Here, he practiced his writing skills and first adopted the name Mark Twain, a name that would soon be known throughout the world.

36 FACTS

* Hoover Dam is located in Nevada. It's one of the highest dams in the world.

* Nevada may be ranked 7th in land area, but 85% of it is owned by the Federal Government.

* Nevada is mostly desert, but did you know that the Sierra Nevada mountain range has areas that are covered in snow for six months of the year? It's true.

* Nevada got its name from a Spanish word that means "snow-clad."

THE SILVER STATE. Nevada is rich in silver, but the mining of gold is going strong too. So stong, in fact, that if Nevada was its own country, it would rank 2nd in the world; only South Africa produces more.

Note: From 1870 to 1893, gold and silver coins were minted in Carson City, Nevada. Only eight American cities have ever minted coins.

NV

GEOQUIZ

STATES	CAPITALS	BORDERS	TRIVIA
	My capital is SPRINGFIELD	I border Kentucky and Wisconsin.	I am called the LAND OF 10,000 LAKES.
PAGE 41	PAGE 21	PAGE 21	PAGE 33

39

40

NEW HAMPSHIRE
CAPITAL: Concord
STATEHOOD: June 21, 1788

Population: 1,281,000 RANK: 42nd	Area: 8,969 square miles RANK: 44th

Manchester Nashua Concord

A LAND OF ALL SEASONS.
New Hampshire is known for its changeable climate. With its proximity to mountains, lakes, rivers, and the ocean, the state experiences the splendor of all four seasons. The winters are cold and long, ideal for skiing; the summers are short and cool; and falls are the perfect pictures of the glory of foliage. Each year, many come to New Hampshire to enjoy the beauty of nature.

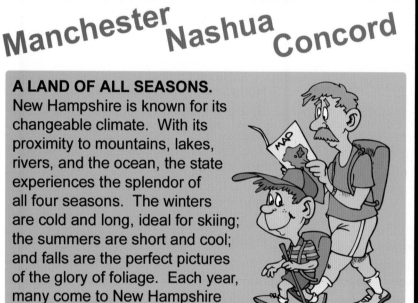

9 FACTS

* "Live Free or Die," the state motto of New Hampshire, expresses its Revolutionary War sentiments.

* Captain John Smith gave New Hampshire its name. He named it in honor of Hampshire, his hometown in England.

* Mount Washington is considered to be America's windiest place. On April 12th, 1934, a wind of 234 miles per hour was measured there.

* Alan Shepard, Jr. was born in New Hampshire. He was the first American in space.

"LIVE FREE OR DIE." Of the thirteen colonies, New Hampshire was the first to declare its independence from England. Later, when the representatives of the thirteen colonies assembled to vote for the Declaration of Independence, the delegates from New Hampshire were given the honor of casting their votes first. That date was July 4th, 1776.

NH

GEOQUIZ

STATES	CAPITALS	BORDERS	TRIVIA
PAGE 52	My capital is OKLAHOMA CITY PAGE 48	I border only two states: Georgia and North Carolina. PAGE 53	I am called the GRAND CANYON State. PAGE 8

NEW JERSEY

CAPITAL: Trenton

STATEHOOD: December 18, 1787

Population: 8,392,000 RANK: 10th

Area: 7,418 square miles RANK: 46th

Newark Jersey City Paterson

ELBOW ROOM? If you're looking for space, then New Jersey isn't the place. With over 1,100 people living per square mile, this East Coast state is easily the most densely populated. And because of this, it isn't too surprising to learn that 90% of New Jersians live in urban areas and that every New Jersey county is classified as a metropolitan area. What keeps the state going? Well, New Jersey is a leading industrial and chemical-producing state.

3 FACTS

* New Jersey is called the Garden State.

* President Grover Cleveland was from New Jersey. The only man to serve two nonconsecutive terms in the White House, he was the 22nd *and* 24th President.

* Some other famous New Jersians include: political leader Aaron Burr, explorer Zebulon Pike, entertainer Jerry Lewis, and General Norman Schwarzkopf.

* Wow, the Statue of Liberty is NOT in New York. It's in New Jersey.

THE CROSSROADS. New Jersey played a pivotal role during the Revolutionary War. Geographically, the state was practically in the center of the nation; therefore, it was common to see both British and American troops crisscrossing the state between New York and Pennsylvania. In fact, because of its strategic location, New Jersey was the setting for more battles than any other state.

GEOQUIZ

STATES	CAPITALS	BORDERS	TRIVIA
	My capital is SAINT PAUL	I border Ohio and Wisconsin.	Helen Keller was from this state.
PAGE 22	PAGE 33	PAGE 32	PAGE 6

NEW MEXICO

CAPITAL: Santa Fe

STATEHOOD: January 6, 1912

Population: 2,016,000	Area: 121,355 square miles
RANK: 36th	RANK: 5th

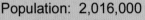

Albuquerque   Las Cruces   Santa Fe

BEWARE, THE NIGHT.

Carlsbad Cavern is an attraction like no other. With nearly one million bats calling the sanctuary their home, the moonlit sky often becomes darkened when these creatures take to flight. One chamber in the cavern is especially huge. It's over ten football fields long and more than twenty stories high!

47 FACTS

* Did you think Denver was high? Well, at 7,000 feet above sea level, New Mexico's Santa Fe is the highest capital in America.

* BOOM! The world's first atomic bomb was detonated at the White Sands Testing Area in 1945. The development of this weapon helped to shorten the Second World War.

* Did you know that New Mexico's constitution states that it's a bilingual state? Nearly 1 in 3 citizens of New Mexico speaks Spanish at home.

NOT MUCH WATER. New Mexico is a very dry state, with less than 1% of its surface area being lakes and rivers. Nonetheless, the desert state has some beautiful scenery. White Sands National Monument is considered a desert, but it's not one made of sand. White gypsum crystals produce gleaming effects that attract many visitors to the wonders of New Mexico.

NM

GEOQUIZ

STATES	CAPITALS	BORDERS	TRIVIA
	My capital is RALEIGH	I form Utah's WESTERN border.	I am home to Little Bighorn.
PAGE 35	PAGE 45	PAGE 39	PAGE 36

NEW YORK

CAPITAL: Albany
STATEHOOD: July 26, 1788

Population: 18,250,000	Area: 47,223 square miles
RANK: 3rd	RANK: 30th

New York City   Buffalo   Rochester

ELEVATORS AND SUBWAYS.
New York City is by far the largest city in the United States. With 8.5 million people, it more than doubles the next largest city, Los Angeles. Now, because of its huge buildings and dense population, elevators and subways have become common forms of transportation. In fact, New York City has over 700 miles of subway track to take people from one part of the city to another.

11   FACTS

* New York was named in honor of the Duke of York.

* The first railroad in the United States was built in New York. It connected Schenectady to Albany.

* Did you know that New York City once served as our nation's capital?

* The headquarters for the United Nations are in New York.

* Presidents Martin Van Buren, Millard Fillmore, Theodore Roosevelt and Franklin Roosevelt were from New York.

A SAD DAY. Almost 100 years before the World Trade Center tragedies, New York City dealt with a disaster aboard the excursion ferry "The General Slocum." On June 15th, 1904, the ferry caught fire with 1,358 people on board; most of them were women and children going to a church picnic. Before lifeboats could be lowered, the wooden boat was ablaze and passengers were trapped beneath the decks. In all, 1,021 people died.

GEOQUIZ

STATES	CAPITALS	BORDERS	TRIVIA
I am not Colorado.	My capital is AUGUSTA	I border Maine and Massachusetts.	I was the first state to allow women to vote.
PAGE 66	PAGE 28	PAGE 40	PAGE 66

GROWTH RATE

The U.S. is still growing. From 2000 to 2005, our nation has grown by 5.3%, but are any states growing faster than others? Yes! As this map illustrates, western states and southern states along the Atlantic Ocean are experiencing the largest growth rates. The RED states (Florida, Georgia, Arizona, Utah, Nevada, and Idaho) are leading the way with more than 10% growth. The only areas which are believed to have experienced a population decline (in BLUE) are North Dakota and Washington, D.C.

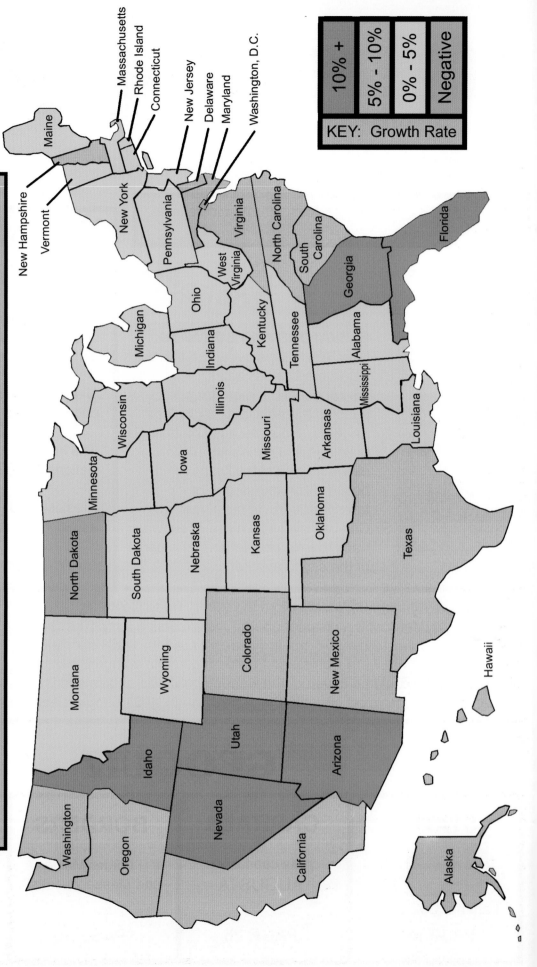

KEY: Growth Rate

| 10% + | 5% - 10% | 0% - 5% | Negative |

NORTH CAROLINA

CAPITAL: Raleigh
STATEHOOD: November 21, 1789

Population: 8,227,000	Area: 48,718 square miles
RANK: 11th	RANK: 29th

Charlotte Raleigh Greensboro

The Wright Brothers

IT'S A BIRD... In 1903, Orville and Wilbur Wright made history by being the first men to successfully make a powered flight with an airplane. About four miles outside Kitty Hawk, the brothers took to the air on a sand mountain near the ocean. And although Kitty Hawk is often credited with being the location of this event, the actual location was at Kill Devil's Hill. Kitty Hawk was merely the place where Orville sent a telegraph containing news of their flight.

12 FACTS

* North Carolina is commonly known as the Tarheel State.

* Presidents Andrew Johnson and James K. Polk were from North Carolina.

* Other famous North Carolinians include: First Lady Dolley Madison, Revolutionary War soldier Braxton Bragg, auto racer Richard Petty, and evangelist Billy Graham.

* On March 7th, 1914, Babe Ruth hit his first professional homerun. He was playing in Fayetteville, North Carolina at the time.

LEADING THE NATION. North Carolina is first in the nation in its production of sweet potatoes, tobacco, brick, furniture, and textiles. The state also has the distinction of being the site of England's first colony in America. Sadly, however, the colony didn't survive. In fact, all the colonists of Roanoke Island mysteriously disappeared around 1590. The only clue as to their whereabouts was the word "Croatoan." It was found etched on a log.

NC

GEOQUIZ

STATES	CAPITALS	BORDERS	TRIVIA
	My capital is MONTGOMERY	I border Texas and Arizona.	Abraham Lincoln and Jefferson Davis were born in this state.
PAGE 33	PAGE 6	PAGE 42	PAGE 26

NORTH DAKOTA

CAPITAL: Bismarck
STATEHOOD: November 2, 1889

Population: 677,000
RANK: 48th

Area: 68,994 square miles
RANK: 17th

Fargo Bismarck Grand Forks

SACAGAWEA. America can appreciate the efforts of this Shoshone Indian girl. In 1804, when Lewis and Clark traveled through the area that's now North Dakota, they were able to procure her services as an interpreter and guide. But Sacagawea went above and beyond her duties. Not only did she point out the safest foods to eat, she rescued books, papers, instruments, and medicines when a boat capsized during a storm. Lewis and Clark frequently praised her for her service.

39 40 FACTS

* North Dakota is home to North America's geographic center.

* North Dakota leads the nation in its production of sunflowers.

* Did you know that North Dakota has many dinosaur fossils hidden under its soil? It's an archeological gold mine.

* North Dakota is called the Flickertail State, but what does that mean? Flickertail is another name for the Richardson ground squirrel. While running, the furry native of North Dakota sometimes flicks its tail.

WHICH STATE IS IT? Was North Dakota the 39th or 40th state to be admitted to the Union? No one really knows. On November 2nd, 1889, it and South Dakota entered the Union at exactly the same time. Therefore, when you read about either of the Dakota states, you'll find statements like "39th or 40th" attached to them.

ND

GEOQUIZ

STATES	CAPITALS	BORDERS	TRIVIA
	My capital is MADISON	New Hampshire and Vermont form my NORTHERN border.	This state is home to O'Hare, the busiest airport in the world.
PAGE 58	PAGE 65	PAGE 30	PAGE 21

OHIO

CAPITAL: Columbus
STATEHOOD: March 1, 1803

Population: 11,428,000	Area: 40,953 square miles
RANK: 7th	RANK: 35th

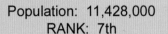

Columbus Cleveland Cincinnati

ORGANIZED SPORTS. Ohioans can take pride in the fact that they helped start the growth of professional sports. In 1869, the Cincinnati Red Stockings took the field as America's first pro baseball team. That team won its first 130 games before falling to the Brooklyn Atlantics, 8-7. Also, in 1920, the first professional football league was formed in Canton, Ohio. During that year, the Akron Pros finished the season with six wins, no losses, and three ties.

17 FACTS

* Cleveland, Ohio was the first city in the world to be lighted with electricity.

* In 1924, Ohio's DeHart Hubbard became the first African-American to win an Olympic gold medal.

* Cleveland's Jesse Owens also won Olympic gold. In 1936, he brought home four gold medals!

* Do you live within 500 miles of Columbus, Ohio? Nearly half the people in our nation do.

* Ohio is called the Buckeye State.

ALL OR NOTHING. It's hard to believe, but seven presidents have come from the state of Ohio. They are: Ulysses S. Grant, Rutherford B. Hayes, James A. Garfield, Benjamin Harrison, William McKinley, William H. Taft, and Warren G. Harding. However, despite these lofty numbers, Ohio never produced any of the forty-five vice presidents who served our nation.

OH

GEOQUIZ

STATES	CAPITALS	BORDERS	TRIVIA
	My capital is COLUMBIA	Oregon forms my SOUTHERN border.	I am called the GEM State.
PAGE 18	PAGE 53	PAGE 62	PAGE 20

48

OKLAHOMA

CAPITAL: Oklahoma City
STATEHOOD: November 16, 1907

Population: 3,491,000   Area: 68,679 square miles
RANK: 28th   RANK: 19th

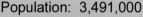
Oklahoma City Tulsa Norman

A REAL CHAMPION. Born in a one-room cabin in 1887, Jim Thorpe grew up to become a track, baseball, and football star. When he competed in the 1912 Olympics, he won four gold medals and the praises of Belgium's King Gustav V. "Sir," the king said, "you are the greatest athlete in the world!" To this day, there are few who would disagree.

NOTE: Jim Thorpe had a twin brother, Charlie, who died of pneumonia at the age of 8.

46 FACTS

* Choctaw was established in 1893. It's Oklahoma's oldest town.

* Did you know that Boise City was the only U.S. city to be bombed during World War II? That's right. On July 5th, 1943, the U.S. military dropped some "practice" bombs on the city.

* Oklahoma City is home to the National Cowboy Hall of Fame.

* In 1935, the nation's first parking meter was installed in Oklahoma City.

 **THE SOONER STATE?** April 22nd, 1889, was the date that the U.S. Government opened much of Oklahoma for settlement, and 50,000 people gathered to await the start of the "race" for land. However, prior to the sounding of the noonday gun, some started "sooner" than the others. Hence, the state got its nickname.

 OK

GEOQUIZ

STATES	CAPITALS	BORDERS	TRIVIA
	My capital is BATON ROUGE	I border Nebraska and North Dakota.	I am called the FLICKERTAIL State.
PAGE 15	PAGE 27	PAGE 54	PAGE 46

OREGON

CAPITAL: Salem
STATEHOOD: February 14, 1859

Population: 3,613,000	Area: 96,003 square miles
RANK: 27th	RANK: 10th

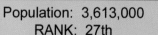
Portland Salem Eugene

BOO! No, Oregon doesn't have the most ghosts, but it does claim to have the most ghost towns! Many towns, like Yellow Dog and Raw Dog, were doomed to perish when newly-built roads made stagecoach stops unnecessary. Others faded when gold could no longer be found, and then there's the story of Antelope. First hit by a fire, the rebuilt town faded into history when a railroad station was built in a nearby town.

33 FACTS

* The deepest lake in America is Oregon's Crater Lake. It's the remains of an ancient volcano.

* Oregon is also home to America's deepest canyon. It's over 8,000 feet deep!

* Oregon has a nickname. It's called the Beaver State.

* The word *Oregon* means...? Well, no one really knows the answer to that question. It's unknown.

* Wow! Oregon doesn't have any SELF-service gas stations.

OREGON. During the late 1700s and early 1800s, hunters and trappers pushed westward to Oregon. Here, they found the land teeming with beaver. Companies established themselves, and pioneers soon followed to tame the fertile soil. Afterwards, gold was discovered and even more settlers moved to the area. However, many of them turned to the logging and fishing industries when their search for gold didn't "pan out."

OR

GEOQUIZ

STATES	CAPITALS	BORDERS	TRIVIA
	My capital is CARSON CITY	I border Delaware and Virginia.	I am the birthplace to SEVEN U.S. presidents.
PAGE 42	PAGE 39	PAGE 29	PAGE 47

50

AREA RANKINGS

Which states are the biggest? Which are the smallest? Each state has been listed in order of size on the chart below. As most of you are aware, Alaska is the largest, so it comes first on the list. Now, can you find which state is last on this list? It's Rhode Island. Rhode Island has the least area of all 50 states. But what's that strange number after its name? Well, that's how many times Rhode Island would fit INTO Alaska! That's right, it would take more than 429 Rhode Islands to fit into one Alaska.

1. Alaska	1.00	26. Iowa	11.79
2. Texas	2.47	27. New York	12.16
3. California	4.05	28. North Carolina	12.32
4. Montana	4.51	29. Arkansas	12.47
5. New Mexico	5.45	30. Alabama	12.65
6. Arizona	5.81	31. Louisiana	12.79
7. Nevada	6.00	32. Mississippi	13.69
8. Colorado	6.37	33. Pennsylvania	14.40
9. Oregon	6.74	34. Ohio	14.80
10. Wyoming	6.78	35. Virginia	15.50
11. Michigan	6.85	36. Tennessee	15.74
12. Minnesota	7.63	37. Kentucky	16.41
13. Utah	7.81	38. Indiana	18.21
14. Idaho	7.94	39. Maine	18.74
15. Kansas	8.06	40. South Carolina	20.71
16. Nebraska	8.57	41. West Virginia	27.37
17. South Dakota	8.60	42. Maryland	53.46
18. Washington	9.30	43. Hawaii	60.68
19. North Dakota	9.38	44. Massachusetts	62.85
20. Oklahoma	9.49	45. Vermont	69.99
21. Missouri	9.52	46. New Hampshire	70.94
22. Florida	10.09	47. New Jersey	76.05
23. Wisconsin	10.13	48. Connecticut	119.66
24. Georgia	11.16	49. Delaware	266.48
25. Illinois	11.45	50. Rhode Island	429.30

PENNSYLVANIA

CAPITAL: Harrisburg

STATEHOOD: December 12, 1787

Population: 12,281,000	Area: 44,820 square miles
RANK: 5th	RANK: 32nd

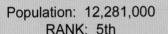

Philadelphia Pittsburgh Allentown

A LEADER. The city of Philadelphia has been instrumental to the growth of our country. In 1776, representatives from the colonies met there, debated, and eventually signed the Declaration of Independence. In 1784, it became the home of our nation's first newspaper. For a time, it served as our nation's capital, and it has the distinction of becoming the first American city to have a zoo. Today, Philadelphia has many historical landmarks that can be visited by those who love history.

2 FACTS

* The *WORDS TO REMEMBER* (shown in purple) come from the Declaration of Independence.

* The nation's first public zoo was founded by Benjamin Franklin in Philadelphia.

* Pennsylvania is named after its founder, William Penn. Many of the democratic principles that he set forth served as an inspiration for the U.S. Constitution.

* Famous Pennsylvanians include: President James Buchanan, explorer Daniel Boone, and Civil War General George McClellan.

WORDS TO REMEMBER. "When in the Course of human Events, it becomes necessary for one People to dissolve the political bands which have connected them with one another, and to assume, among the Powers of the Earth, the separate and equal Station to which the Laws of Nature and of Nature's God entitle them, a decent Respect to the Opinions of Mankind requires that they should declare the Causes which impel them to the Separation."

PA

GEOQUIZ

STATES	CAPITALS	BORDERS	TRIVIA
	My capital is CHEYENNE	I border Missouri and Louisiana.	I am the birthplace of President "Bill" Clinton.
PAGE 11	PAGE 66	PAGE 10	PAGE 10

RHODE ISLAND
CAPITAL: Providence
STATEHOOD: May 29, 1790

Population: 1,012,000	Area: 1,045 square miles
RANK: 43rd	RANK: 50th

Providence Warwick Cranston

MEASURING UP. You bet, when it comes to land size, Rhode Island is the smallest state in the nation. With only 1,045 square miles of land, it would still have to double in size to move up to the 49th spot. But, as history has shown, Rhode Island has been instrumental in American history. In fact, Thomas Jefferson and John Adams acknowledged that Roger Williams, the founder of Rhode Island, was the originator of America's freedom of religion, speech, and public assembly.

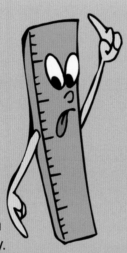

13 FACTS

* Did you know that Rhode Island is called the Ocean State?

* The first British soldiers to fight in the American Revolution landed in Newport.

* America's first African-American regiment fought against the British in Rhode Island.

* America's oldest schoolhouse was built in Portsmouth in 1716.

* Samuel Slater's Rhode Island cotton mill is credited with starting our nation's Industrial Revolution.

A PRELUDE TO WAR. On June 10th, 1772, four years prior to the Revolutionary War, Rhode Islanders were the first to take military action against the English. What did they do? They sunk one of the King's merchant ships, "The Gaspee." A few weeks later, a London newspaper described the incident as the doings of a bunch of smugglers who burned the boat and "carried their commerce in triumph to their own habitations."

RI

GEOQUIZ

STATES	CAPITALS	BORDERS	TRIVIA
	My capital is INDIANAPOLIS	I border Vermont and Pennsylvania.	Las Vegas, Henderson, and Reno are my largest cities.
PAGE 43	PAGE 22	PAGE 43	PAGE 39

SOUTH CAROLINA
CAPITAL: Columbia
STATEHOOD: May 23, 1788

Population: 4,033,000
RANK: 26th

Area: 30,111 square miles
RANK: 40th

8 FACTS

* South Carolina is called the Palmetto State. When the British tried to capture a fort made of Palmetto logs, their cannonballs simply bounced off the spongy wood.

* Does South Carolina have its own Loch Ness monster? Some think that a creature resembling a snake and something prehistoric lives in Lake Murray.

* Famous South Carolinians include: President Andrew Jackson, General Francis Marion, and civil rights leader Jesse Jackson.

CELEBRATIONS. Many don't know it, but Georgia isn't the leading producer of peaches; South Carolina is. Every July, the city of Gaffney hosts a ten-day festival to celebrate the tasty fruit. But the state also has festivals for other delicacies. Ware Shoals has a Catfish Festival; Beaufort hosts a Shrimp Festival; and Little River has a Blue Crab Festival. Then there's the celebration hosted by Myrtle Beach. Every year, it has the Sun Fun Festival.

THE CIVIL WAR. On April 10th, 1861, General Beauregard of the provisional Confederate forces at Charleston demanded the surrender of the Union garrison at Fort Sumter, which was in Charleston Harbor. Union Major Robert Anderson refused to comply and the Confederate batteries opened fire. The Civil War had begun. And although no one died in this first exchange, future battles wouldn't be so bloodless. Over 600,000 would die in the years to come.

sc

GEOQUIZ

STATES	CAPITALS	BORDERS	TRIVIA
	My capital is LINCOLN	I border Michigan and Ohio.	This state was named in honor of one of the presidents.
PAGE 46	PAGE 37	PAGE 22	PAGE 62

SOUTH DAKOTA

CAPITAL: Pierre

STATEHOOD: November 2, 1889

Population: 810,000
RANK: 45th

Area: 75,884 square miles
RANK: 16th

Sioux Falls Rapid City Aberdeen

39 40 FACTS

* South Dakota is home to the world's largest petrified wood park. This area also contains many dinosaur fossils.

* South Dakota is called the Coyote State.

* If you thought Mount Rushmore was big, then just wait until the Crazy Horse mountain project is finished. This sculpture will be 563 feet tall!

* Wind Cave is huge. With nearly 82 miles of passageways, it's quite a tourist attraction.

FAMOUS FACES. Although less than one million people live there, a variety of recognizable names have come from South Dakota: Vice President Hubert Humphrey, TV newscaster Tom Brokaw, baseball manager Sparky Anderson, politician George McGovern, and actress Cheryl Ladd, to name a few.

A BEAUTIFUL CARVING. South Dakota is home to one of America's greatest monuments, Mount Rushmore. The sculpture of George Washington, Thomas Jefferson, Theodore Roosevelt, and Abraham Lincoln draws many tourists each year. The project in honor of these four presidents began in 1927, cost one million dollars, and took sculptor Gutzon Borglum nearly fourteen years to complete.

SD

GEOQUIZ

STATES	CAPITALS	BORDERS	TRIVIA
	My capital is COLUMBUS	Pennsylvania forms most of my WESTERN border.	New Orleans is in this state.
PAGE 62	PAGE 47	PAGE 41	PAGE 27

Where did I see that?

See if you can remember where you saw these pictures before.
ANSWERS ON PAGE 63

1.

2.

3.

4.

5.

6.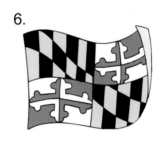

7.

8.

9.

10.

11.

12.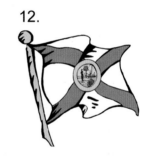

13.

14.

15.

16.

17.

18.

19.

20.

TENNESSEE

CAPITAL: Nashville
STATEHOOD: June 1, 1796

Population: 5,966,000	Area: 41,220 square miles
RANK: 16th	RANK: 34th

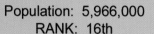

Memphis Nashville Knoxville

THE VOLUNTEER STATE. During the War of 1812, many Tennesseans volunteered to fight against the British. One battle where they served with extreme valor was the Battle of New Orleans. Tennessean Andrew Jackson, who would later become president of the United States, successfully set up defensive positions against the British at this battle. His victory was one key reason for his election and the state's right to be proudly called the Volunteer State.

16 FACTS

* Following the assassination of Abraham Lincoln, Tennessean Andrew Johnson (not Jackson) became president.

* The first female U.S. senator was from Tennessee. Her name was Hattie Caraway.

* Jackson was the home of Casey Jones, the famous railroad engineer who died when his train crashed in 1900.

* The Great Smoky Mountains National Park is the most visited national park in America.

COUNTRY MUSIC CAPITAL OF THE WORLD. Nashville, Tennessee is home to The Grand Ole Opry, a centerpiece for country music singers. Since 1925, the musical theater has been broadcasting on the radio every Friday and Saturday night (a record for the airwaves). Some of the names that have made the Opry famous are: Uncle Dave Macon, Minnie Pearl, Eddy Arnold, and Pee Wee King.

TN

GEOQUIZ

STATES	CAPITALS	BORDERS	TRIVIA
	My capital is DOVER	I form New Hampshire's EASTERN border.	I am called the HOOSIER State.
PAGE 23	PAGE 15	PAGE 28	PAGE 22

TEXAS

CAPITAL: Austin

STATEHOOD: December 29, 1845

Population: 21,487,000   Area: 261,914 square miles
RANK: 2nd   RANK: 2nd

Houston San Antonio Dallas

THE LONE STAR. In the early 1800s, Texas was part of Mexico and many Americans had settled there. Fearing that the influx of foreigners would lead to rebellion, Mexico forbade further immigration of Americans into Texas. This policy infuriated American-born Texans, led to a few skirmishes, and sent the land into war by 1835. With the help of Sam Bowie, Davy Crockett, Sam Houston, William Travis, and Stephen Austin, Texas won its independence and became its own country. That's right, its own *country*! But this didn't last long. In 1845, Texas joined the United States by becoming the 28th state.

28 FACTS

* Texas is called the Lone Star State.

* Presidents Lyndon B. Johnson and Dwight D. Eisenhower were born in Texas.

* President George Bush and his son, President George W. Bush, are residents of Texas.

* Texas' King Ranch is big, big, big! In fact, it's bigger than the whole state of Rhode Island!

* In 1900, over 8,000 died when a hurricane struck Galveston. It was our nation's worst natural disaster.

 **BLACK GOLD!** Texas has oil and lots of it. In 2004, the state produced over one million barrels a day, making it the number one producing state. As a whole, the nation pumped out 5.4 million barrels a day. Therefore, with Texas bringing in nearly 20% of the nation's crude, we can be thankful that it's no longer its own country!

TX

GEOQUIZ

STATES	CAPITALS	BORDERS	TRIVIA
	My capital is LITTLE ROCK	I border California and New Mexico.	I am called the GARDEN State.
PAGE 8	PAGE 10	PAGE 8	PAGE 41

UTAH

CAPITAL: Salt Lake City
STATEHOOD: January 4, 1896

Population: 2,411,000
RANK: 34th

Area: 82,168 square miles
RANK: 12th

Salt Lake City
West Valley City
Provo

THE MEETING POINT. Prior to the invention of the car and the making of highways, the necessity of creating a railroad to bridge the gap between America's east and west coast was a priority. On May 10th, 1869, this project was completed in what is now Utah. Silver and gold spikes were driven into the last rail to honor this great event.

45 FACTS

* Brigham Young led the first group of non-native Americans to the land that is now Utah.

* Utah is called the <u>Beehive</u> State, but not because of its insect population. No, the symbol merely represents the diligence and thrift of Utah's citizens.

* A+. Utah has the highest literacy rate in America.

* In 2002, the XIX Winter Olympic Games were held in Utah, where yearly snowfall can surpass 500 inches in the mountains.

A UNIQUE PLACE. Utah's Great Salt Lake is very special. Although it covers more than 2,100 square miles, the huge lake only has an average depth of 13 feet! But, if anything sets this lake apart from others, it's the saltiness of the water. With a salinity of nearly 12%, the Great Salt Lake is MUCH saltier than the ocean. In fact, it's so salty that people can easily stay afloat.

GEOQUIZ

STATES	CAPITALS	BORDERS	TRIVIA
	My capital is CHARLESTON	I border Georgia and Kentucky.	Captain John Smith named this state in honor of his English hometown.
PAGE 24	PAGE 64	PAGE 56	PAGE 40

VERMONT

CAPITAL: Montpelier

STATEHOOD: March 4, 1791

Population: 638,000	Area: 9,249 square miles
RANK: 49th	RANK: 43rd

Burlington Rutland South Burlington

RICH IN BEAUTY. Vermont is called the Green Mountain State for good reason. It has over 220 mountains that exceed 2,000 feet in elevation! Snow skiing is very popular in the state, as vacationers from around the country come in droves to enjoy the slopes that await. But tourism isn't Vermont's only means of surviving: the state is the nation's leading producer of maple syrup; it supplies half the milk that New Englanders consume; and it produces large amounts of apples, potatoes, honey, and lumber.

14 FACTS

* Vermont's state motto is: "Freedom and Unity."

* Famous Vermonters include: President Chester Arthur, President Calvin Coolidge, Admiral George Dewey, and religious leader Brigham Young.

* With under 10,000 people, Montpelier is America's least populated state capital.

* Before becoming a state, Vermont was claimed by both New York and New Hampshire.

INDEPENDENT. When speaking of Vermont, the Georgia state legislature once said that "the whole state should be made into an island and towed out to sea." Although the words were meant as an insult, the nation can take pride in many of the ideals that this state holds. For instance, Vermont demonstrated the true meaning of freedom by being the *first* state to outlaw slavery.

Free!

VT

GEOQUIZ

STATES	CAPITALS	BORDERS	TRIVIA
	My capital is OLYMPIA	I border Virginia and South Carolina.	John Wayne and President Herbert Hoover were born in this state.
PAGE 54	PAGE 62	PAGE 45	PAGE 23

Where did I read that?

Here are some clues. See if you can name the states.
ANSWERS ON PAGE 63

21. I am home to Mammoth Cave National Park.
22. Breaking away from Virginia, I became a state in 1863.
23. When it comes to land size, I am the largest state, by far!
24. I was the 50th state to be admitted to the Union.
25. When it comes to people, I have the most.
26. The first public zoo was opened in this state.
27. Corydon used to be my state capital.
28. I am called the Lone Star State.
29. This state normally produces the most CHEESE each year.
30. The site where George Custer had his last stand is in this state.
31. This state usually produces the most PEACHES each year.
32. I am called the Land of 10,000 Lakes.
33. I am home to the Grand Ole Opry.
34. O'Hare International Airport is in this state.
35. You can find the John F. Kennedy Space Center in this state.
36. Albuquerque and Las Cruces are my two largest cities.
37. I was the birthplace to EIGHT U.S. presidents, including Thomas Jefferson.
38. The Declaration of Independence was signed in this state.
39. Detroit and Grand Rapids can be found in this state.
40. I am called the Peach State.
41. The Great Salt Lake can be found here.
42. The Wright Brothers made the first heavier-than-air flight in this state.
43. I am called the Cornhusker State.
44. I am home to Mount Saint Helens, a volcano.
45. I am called the Gem State, but my potatoes are probably better known.
46. SEVEN U.S. presidents were born in this state, including Ulysses S. Grant.
47. I am called the Flickertail State. I'm either the 39th or 40th state.
48. My Pike's Peak inspired Katharine Bates' "purple mountains majesty" phrase.
49. This state is home to the most populated city in America.
50. Jackson, Gulfport, and Biloxi are the three largest cities in this state.

TIME OUT!
If you're wondering, the first twenty clues are on page 55.

VIRGINIA

CAPITAL: Richmond
STATEHOOD: June 25, 1788

Population: 7,324,000 RANK: 12th	Area: 39,598 square miles RANK: 37th

Virginia Beach Norfolk Chesapeake

BATTLE-TESTED. Virginia has been the field of many battles. In 1781, during the Revolutionary War, Yorktown was the site of Lord Cornwallis' defeat to George Washington. Then, years later, Confederate General Robert E. Lee was defeated by the Union army during the Civil War. With each of these surrenders, our nation was able to witness the end of two major wars.

10 FACTS

* Virginia was named in honor of England's Queen Elizabeth I.

* Famous Virginians include: Henry Clay, Robert E. Lee, Sam Houston, Booker T. Washington, Patrick Henry, and Nat Turner.

* In addition to being called the Old Dominion State, Virginia is called the Mother of States. Why? Well, West Virginia, Ohio, Kentucky, Indiana, Illinois, Wisconsin, and parts of Minnesota were all once part of Virginia.

* Tobacco is Virginia's major cash crop.

EIGHT IS ENOUGH? Virginia is often referred to as the Mother of Presidents because eight Virginians have held the highest post in the land. They are: George Washington, Thomas Jefferson, James Madison, James Monroe, William Henry Harrison, John Tyler, Zachary Taylor, and Woodrow Wilson. The only other state that's close to Virginia's record is Ohio with seven presidents.

 VA

GEOQUIZ

STATES	CAPITALS	BORDERS	TRIVIA
	My capital is PIERRE	I border Missouri and Minnesota.	The miner '49ers came here to search for gold.
PAGE 6	PAGE 54	PAGE 23	PAGE 11

WASHINGTON

CAPITAL: Olympia
STATEHOOD: November 11, 1889

Population: 6,258,000 RANK: 14th	Area: 66,582 square miles RANK: 20th

Seattle   Spokane   Tacoma

OUTDOOR FUN. If you like outdoor adventure, Washington is the place to be. Whitewater rafting is a year-round sport, with spring runoff of mountain snow and steady amounts of rain continually feeding the state's many rivers. But, if that isn't your idea of fun, you could always try one of the state's other popular activities: hiking, camping, mountainbiking, fishing, skiing, snowboarding, horseback riding, or kayaking. No doubt, Washington has it all!

42 FACTS

* As its state flag suggests, Washington was named in honor of our nation's first president.

* Washington's highest point is Mount Rainier. It was named after Peter Rainier, a British soldier.

* Medina is the home of Bill Gates, the wealthiest man in the world.

* Washington's King County was originally named after Vice President William King. However, in 1986, it was renamed in honor of civil rights leader Dr. Martin Luther King.

A SLEEPING GIANT. Lewis and Clark described Mount Saint Helens as "perhaps the greatest pinnacle in America," but many local Indians avoided the sleeping volcano, calling it by a name meaning "fire mountain." On May 18th, 1990, the "fire mountain" came to life. After the mountain's north side gave way, a 500-degree cloud of smoke and ash killed everything within 10 miles of the north side.

WA

GEOQUIZ

STATES	CAPITALS	BORDERS	TRIVIA
PAGE 47	My capital is JEFFERSON CITY PAGE 35	CONGRATULATIONS! You have completed the BORDERS challenge.	Albuquerque is the largest city in this state. PAGE 42

QUIZ ANSWERS

WHERE DID I SEE THAT?

(Test on page 55)

1. Oregon
2. Kansas
3. New Jersey
4. South Carolina
5. Nevada
6. Maryland
7. Wyoming
8. Pennsylvania
9. California
10. Alabama
11. Arkansas
12. Florida
13. Colorado
14. Arizona
15. Hawaii
16. Kansas
17. West Virginia
18. Delaware
19. Montana
20. Wisconsin

WHERE DID I READ THAT?

(Test on page 60)

21. Kentucky
22. West Virginia
23. Alaska
24. Hawaii
25. California
26. Pennsylvania
27. Indiana
28. Texas
29. Wisconsin
30. Montana
31. South Carolina
32. Minnesota
33. Tennessee
34. Illinois
35. Florida
36. New Mexico
37. Virginia
38. Pennsylvania
39. Michigan
40. Georgia
41. Utah
42. North Carolina
43. Nebraska
44. Washington
45. Idaho
46. Ohio
47. North Dakota
48. Colorado
49. New York
50. Mississippi

Are you ready for a
GEOQUIZ?

Jump over to page 5
and give it a try!

WEST VIRGINIA

CAPITAL: Charleston
STATEHOOD: June 20, 1863

Population: 1,849,000
RANK: 37th

Area: 24,087 square miles
RANK: 41st

Charleston Huntington Parkersburg

COAL. The economy of West Virginia and the nation depends heavily upon the ability to mine coal that hides beneath the soil. With that in mind, West Virginia is a leader in this endeavor, accounting for nearly 15% of the nation's coal and 50% of U.S. coal exports.

NOTE: More than half our nation's electricity is generated from coal.

35 FACTS

* In 1870, the first brick street in the world was laid in Charleston.

* West Virginian Chester Merriman was the youngest American to serve during World War I. He was only fourteen years old when he enlisted.

* The Golden Delicious Apple had its beginning in Clay County, West Virginia.

* On July 1st, 1921, West Virginia became the first state to institute a sales tax.

THE GREAT SPLIT. West Virginia became a state during the Civil War after it broke away from the Confederate state of Virginia. By proclamation, President Lincoln paved the way for the citizens of Virginia's western area (who mostly sympathized with the North) to gain their sovereignty and become part of the Union. Because of this, West Virginia is sometimes called the northernmost southern state and the southernmost northern state.

GEOQUIZ

STATES	CAPITALS	BORDERS	TRIVIA
	My capital is JACKSON	South Dakota forms my SOUTHERN border.	I am home to the largest city in the U.S.
PAGE 59	PAGE 34	PAGE 46	PAGE 43

WISCONSIN

CAPITAL: Madison
STATEHOOD: May 29, 1848

Population: 5,479,000	Area: 54,314 square miles
RANK: 18th	RANK: 25th

Milwaukee Madison Green Bay

WHAT WAS THAT? Over the years, Wisconsin has come to be regarded as the UFO capital of the Midwest. Sightings of saucers flying through the air and even balls of light bobbing in nearby lakes have been reported. But, although there's no proof of extraterrestrial life forms existing, who could blame them for visiting Wisconsin if they did? It's a great place to visit if you're in the Milky Way.

30 FACTS

* Wisconsin's motto is simple, yet meaningful: "Forward."

* Did you know that if you lined up all Wisconsin's streams and rivers, they would stretch around the world?

* In 1854, the Republican Party was founded in Ripon, Wisconsin.

* Famous Wisconsinites include: magician Harry Houdini, circus greats Charles and John Ringling, actor Spencer Tracy, and Supreme Court Justice William Rehnquist.

THE FACTS. With over 44% of Wisconsin's land being owned by farmers, the state has become a huge food producer. In recent years, the Badger State has produced over 2.5 billion pounds of cheese annually. No, not 2.5 million pounds, but 2.5 BILLION. Still, dairy products aren't Wisconsin's only claim to fame. The farming state is also a strong leader in its production of cranberries, ginseng, and beans.

GEOQUIZ

STATES	CAPITALS	BORDERS	TRIVIA
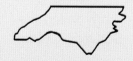 PAGE 45	My capital is DES MOINES PAGE 23	Oklahoma forms my ENTIRE southern border. PAGE 24	Amelia Earhart was from this state. PAGE 24

WYOMING

CAPITAL: Cheyenne
STATEHOOD: July 10, 1890

Population: 568,000	Area: 97,105 square miles
RANK: 50th	RANK: 9th

Cheyenne Casper Laramie

OLD FAITHFUL. Yellowstone National Park (America's first national park) is mostly in the state of Wyoming. When people visit, one of their favorite stops is Old Faithful Geyser, just one of a number of hot springs that frequent the park. Erupting from 18 to 21 times a day, the mammoth geyser discharges nearly 7,000 gallons of water each time. The blasts last less than a minute and end with a few puffs of steam.

44 FACTS

* With under 600,000 people, Wyoming is the least-populated state in the nation.

* Someone from Wyoming is called a Wyomingite.

* Before the Europeans arrived, the land which was to become Wyoming was teeming with bison.

* In 1906, Wyoming's Devils Tower became our nation's first national monument.

* The coal industry is very important to Wyoming's economy.

THE EQUALITY STATE. You have to hand it to Wyoming; it was the first state to grant women the right to vote in elections. Even as far back as 1869, when Wyoming was a mere territory, women had the right to cast ballots.

NOTE: The 19th Amendment to the Constitution was passed in 1920. This guaranteed that women had the same rights as men regarding the right to vote.

WY

GEOQUIZ

STATES	CAPITALS	BORDERS	TRIVIA
	My capital is HELENA	I border Indiana and Pennsylvania.	I am called the SOONER State.
PAGE 32	PAGE 36	PAGE 47	PAGE 48

What's Wrong With This?

Some of these statements are wrong.
Do you know which?

1. Charleston is West Virginia's capital.

2. Texas is called the Lone Star State.

3. Billings is the largest city in Nebraska.

4. The Statue of Liberty is in New York.

5. Hawaii was the 50th state to join the Union.

6. Connecticut is called the Centennial State.

7. Elvis Presley was born in Mississippi.

8. Mount Rushmore is in South Dakota.

9. Virginia is sometimes called the "Mother of States."

10. Wyoming was the first state to give women the right to vote.

11. Alaska could hold over 1,000 states the size of Rhode Island.

12. During the Civil War, Iowa Missouri, and Arkansas fought for the Confederacy.

13. Phoenix is Arizona's capital.

14. Vermont was one of the original 13 Colonies.

15. Pearl Harbor is in Hawaii.

16. President Ronald Reagan was born in California.

17. MI is the abbreviation for Mississippi.

18. Kansas usually has more tornadoes than any other state.

19. The Pilgrims landed in what is now Massachusetts.

20. The Wright Brothers first flew an airplane in South Carolina.

These statements are INCORRECT: 3, 4, 6, 11, 12, 14, 16, 17, 18, 20.

THE 50 STATES

ARE YOU UP TO THE CHALLENGE?

See if you can locate all 50 states on this map. Flip to page 4 to see if you're right.

1. Alabama
2. Alaska
3. Arizona
4. Arkansas
5. California
6. Colorado
7. Connecticut
8. Delaware
9. Florida
10. Georgia
11. Hawaii
12. Idaho
13. Illinois
14. Indiana
15. Iowa
16. Kansas
17. Kentucky
18. Louisiana
19. Maine
20. Maryland
21. Massachusetts
22. Michigan
23. Minnesota
24. Mississippi
25. Missouri

26. Montana
27. Nebraska
28. Nevada
29. New Hampshire
30. New Jersey
31. New Mexico
32. New York
33. North Carolina
34. North Dakota
35. Ohio
36. Oklahoma
37. Oregon
38. Pennsylvania
39. Rhode Island
40. South Carolina
41. South Dakota
42. Tennessee
43. Texas
44. Utah
45. Vermont
46. Virginia
47. Washington
48. West Virginia
49. Wisconsin
50. Wyoming

WASHINGTON, D.C.
Our Nation's Capital Since June 11, 1800

DC

Population: 529,000   Area: 68 square miles

To be. President George Washington didn't live in what is now Washington, D.C. He lived in Philadelphia. However, in 1791, he did choose the site that became our new capital. Believe it or not, it was a marshy swamp! By 1800, his plans for a new capital city were complete, and our second president, John Adams, moved in.

FACTS

* Check out the strange flag! Like individual states, the 68 square miles of land where our nation's capital rests has its own banner. The red, white, and blue flag that you're used to seeing is the symbol of our *entire* nation.

* Before Washington, D.C. became our nation's capital, New York City held the honor.

* The *D.C.* in Washington, D.C. stands for the District of Columbia, with Columbia referring to Christopher Columbus. *Washington* represents George Washington.

Fire. Our president lives in the White House. But did you know that the *first* Washington, D.C. home of our Commander-in-Chief was burned to the ground? That's right! During the War of 1812, the British invaded our nation's new capital city and torched the president's home. Fortunately, President James Madison got away.

Gobble, gobble? Upset with the choice of the bald eagle as our national symbol, Benjamin Franklin said: "The bald eagle is a bird of bad moral character; like those among men who live by robbing, he is generally poor, and often very lousy. The *turkey* is a much more respectable bird and withal a true original native of America." In the end, the eagle's fierce desire to be independent best symbolized the spirit of America.

Laws. Washington, D.C. is also the home of the Capitol. This magnificent building is where our senators and representatives meet to propose new laws. Like the home of the president, it too was burned during the War of 1812. In 1815, the task of rebuilding it started, and the project wasn't completed until 1830.

About the Author:

Joel King is a home school dad with a passion for writing Christian fiction and creating educational resources with unique twists. He loves to play games with his three boys and believes that children retain knowledge better when they are having fun. Joel has a B.S. degree in accounting from the University of Kentucky and works as a state auditor. He lives with his wife and three boys in western Kentucky where they have home schooled their children for six years.

QUICK ORDER FORM

Would you like your own copy? Or perhaps the Workbook that turns this State Book into a 36-week curriculum, chock full of games, puzzles, fill-in-the-blank exercises and maps. Simply indicate the products that interest you and get in touch with us in one of the ways below.

☐ Star-Spangled State Book (the one you hold in your hands) - $18.95
☐ Star-Spangled Workbook + reproducible CD - $34.95
☐ Or request a free catalog and sampler CD which contains samples and entire ebooks which represent our line of quality history and geography resources meant to educate and entertain your students.

Fax Orders: Fax this form to (210)568-9655
Telephone Orders: Call 1(877)697-8611 toll free with your credit card in hand
Mail Orders: Send this form to:

Knowledge Quest, Inc.
4210 Misty Glade, Ste B
San Antonio, TX 78247
(210)745-0203

Name: ⎯⎯⎯⎯⎯⎯⎯⎯⎯⎯⎯⎯⎯⎯⎯⎯⎯⎯⎯⎯⎯⎯⎯⎯⎯

Address: ⎯⎯⎯⎯⎯⎯⎯⎯⎯⎯⎯⎯⎯⎯⎯⎯⎯⎯⎯⎯⎯⎯

City: ⎯⎯⎯⎯⎯⎯⎯⎯⎯⎯⎯⎯⎯⎯⎯⎯⎯⎯⎯⎯⎯⎯⎯⎯

State: ⎯⎯⎯⎯⎯⎯⎯⎯⎯⎯⎯⎯⎯⎯⎯⎯⎯⎯⎯⎯⎯⎯⎯

Zip: ⎯⎯⎯⎯⎯⎯⎯⎯⎯⎯⎯⎯⎯⎯⎯⎯⎯⎯⎯⎯⎯⎯⎯⎯⎯

Telephone: ⎯⎯⎯⎯⎯⎯⎯⎯⎯⎯⎯⎯⎯⎯⎯⎯⎯⎯⎯⎯

Email: ⎯⎯⎯⎯⎯⎯⎯⎯⎯⎯⎯⎯⎯⎯⎯⎯⎯⎯⎯⎯⎯⎯⎯

Subtotal for books indicated above: ⎯⎯⎯⎯⎯⎯⎯
US Shipping, please add $5 for single title and $2 for additional title: ⎯⎯⎯⎯⎯⎯⎯
Total amount enclosed: ⎯⎯⎯⎯⎯⎯⎯

Payment:

☐ check
☐ credit card (indicate type)

Card number: ⎯⎯⎯⎯⎯⎯⎯⎯⎯⎯⎯⎯⎯⎯⎯⎯⎯⎯⎯⎯

Name on card: ⎯⎯⎯⎯⎯⎯⎯⎯⎯⎯⎯⎯⎯⎯⎯⎯⎯⎯⎯

Expiration date: ⎯⎯⎯⎯⎯⎯⎯⎯⎯⎯⎯⎯⎯⎯⎯⎯⎯

Yes, we do sell wholesale as well. Need to contact us? Send an email to orders@knowledgequestmaps.com or visit us online at www.knowledgequestmaps.com